VISUAL TIMELINES WORLD HISTORY

FROM THE STONE AGE TO THE 21ST CENTURY

ANNE ROONEY

ILLUSTRATED BY
VIOLET TOBACCO

ARCTURUS

WHO'S ON THE COVER?

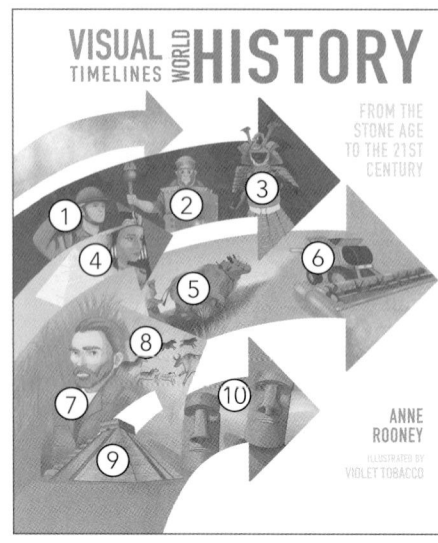

These are the people, animals, and objects on the cover, and a list of pages where you can find more information about them.

1 First World War soldier, page 98
2 Roman legionary, page 40
3 Samurai warrior, page 62
4 Cleopatra, page 39
5 Oxen plow, page 12
6 Combine harvester, page 85
7 Vincent van Gogh, page 90
8 Cave painting, page 10
9 Aztec pyramid, page 65
10 Moai statues, pages 5 and 63

This edition published in 2023 by Arcturus Publishing Limited
26/27 Bickels Yard, 151–153 Bermondsey Street,
London SE1 3HA

Copyright © Arcturus Holdings Limited

Anne Rooney has asserted her right to be identified as the author of this text in accordance with the Copyright, Designs, and Patents Act 1988.

All rights reserved. No part of this publication may be reproduced, stored in a retrieval system, or transmitted, in any form or by any means, electronic, mechanical, photocopying, recording, or otherwise, without prior written permission in accordance with the provisions of the Copyright Act 1956 (as amended).
Any person or persons who do any unauthorized act in relation to this publication may be liable to criminal prosecution and civil claims for damages.

Author: Anne Rooney
Consultants: Ian Fitzgerald and Andrea Page
Illustrator: Violet Tobacco
Designer: Tokiko Morishima
Editors: Becca Clunes and Lucy Doncaster
Design Manager: Jessica Holliland
Editorial Manager: Joe Harris

ISBN: 978-1-3988-1640-4
CH010467US
Supplier 42, Date 0823, PI 00003652

Printed in Singapore

CONTENTS

- 4 **INTRODUCTION**

- 8 **CHAPTER 1: THE BEGINNING OF HISTORY**
- 10 PREHISTORY–11,000 YEARS AGO (9000 BCE)
- 12 8999–3500 BCE
- 14 3499–2500 BCE
- 16 THE START OF HISTORY
- 18 2499–1500 BCE
- 20 CHINESE DYNASTIES
- 22 1499–800 BCE
- 24 799–500 BCE
- 26 FORMS OF GOVERNMENT

- 28 **CHAPTER 2: THE ANCIENT WORLD**
- 30 499–350 BCE
- 32 ALEXANDER THE GREAT
- 34 349–250 BCE
- 36 249–150 BCE
- 38 149–1 BCE
- 40 RISE OF THE ROMAN EMPIRE
- 42 1–250 CE
- 44 251–450 CE
- 46 451–632 CE

- 48 **CHAPTER 3: THE MIDDLE AGES**
- 50 633–749 CE
- 52 LASTING RELIGIONS
- 54 750–849 CE
- 56 850–999 CE
- 58 1000–1099
- 60 MONGOL EMPIRE
- 62 1100–1299
- 64 1300–1399
- 66 BLACK DEATH

- 68 **CHAPTER 4: CONNECTING THE WORLD**
- 70 1400–1484
- 72 1485–1599
- 74 CLOSED WORLDS
- 76 1600–1699
- 78 SELLING HUMANS: SLAVERY
- 80 1700–1799
- 82 INDUSTRIAL REVOLUTION
- 84 1800–1849
- 86 YEAR OF REVOLUTIONS

- 88 **CHAPTER 5: THE WORLD AT WAR**
- 90 1850–1899
- 92 THE INVASION OF AFRICA
- 94 SUFFRAGE
- 96 1900–1919
- 98 THE FIRST WORLD WAR
- 100 1920–1939
- 102 THE SECOND WORLD WAR
- 104 1940–1949
- 106 TYRANTS AND DICTATORS

- 108 **CHAPTER 6: THE MODERN WORLD**
- 110 1950–1964
- 112 THE COLD WAR
- 114 1965–1974
- 116 THE SPACE RACE
- 118 1975–1989
- 120 1990–2004
- 122 2005–PRESENT
- 124 COVID-19
- 126 FUTURE HISTORY

- 128 **INDEX**

INTRODUCTION

Everything that happened before this morning is history! History is the story of the past, of all human activities through time. It covers everything from natural disasters and wars, to inventions, discoveries, and much, much more. History is more than just a string of events, though. One event can cause other things to happen—sometimes unexpectedly—and history slowly builds into patterns. How people respond to an event often determines what happens next. A basic understanding of history is vital to understanding the modern world we live in.

Before history ...

... was prehistory! This was the period when early humans were spreading around the world, then making settlements and building communities. People began to settle and farm the land around 12,000 years ago. This has sometimes been called the "Agricultural Revolution" or the "Neolithic Revolution," and it was a turning point for humans. Farming provided a reliable supply of food, allowing the population to grow. Small settlements eventually grew into cities. People took on specialized types of work, and began to build civilizations with lasting architecture, art, and eventually writing. They began to make history.

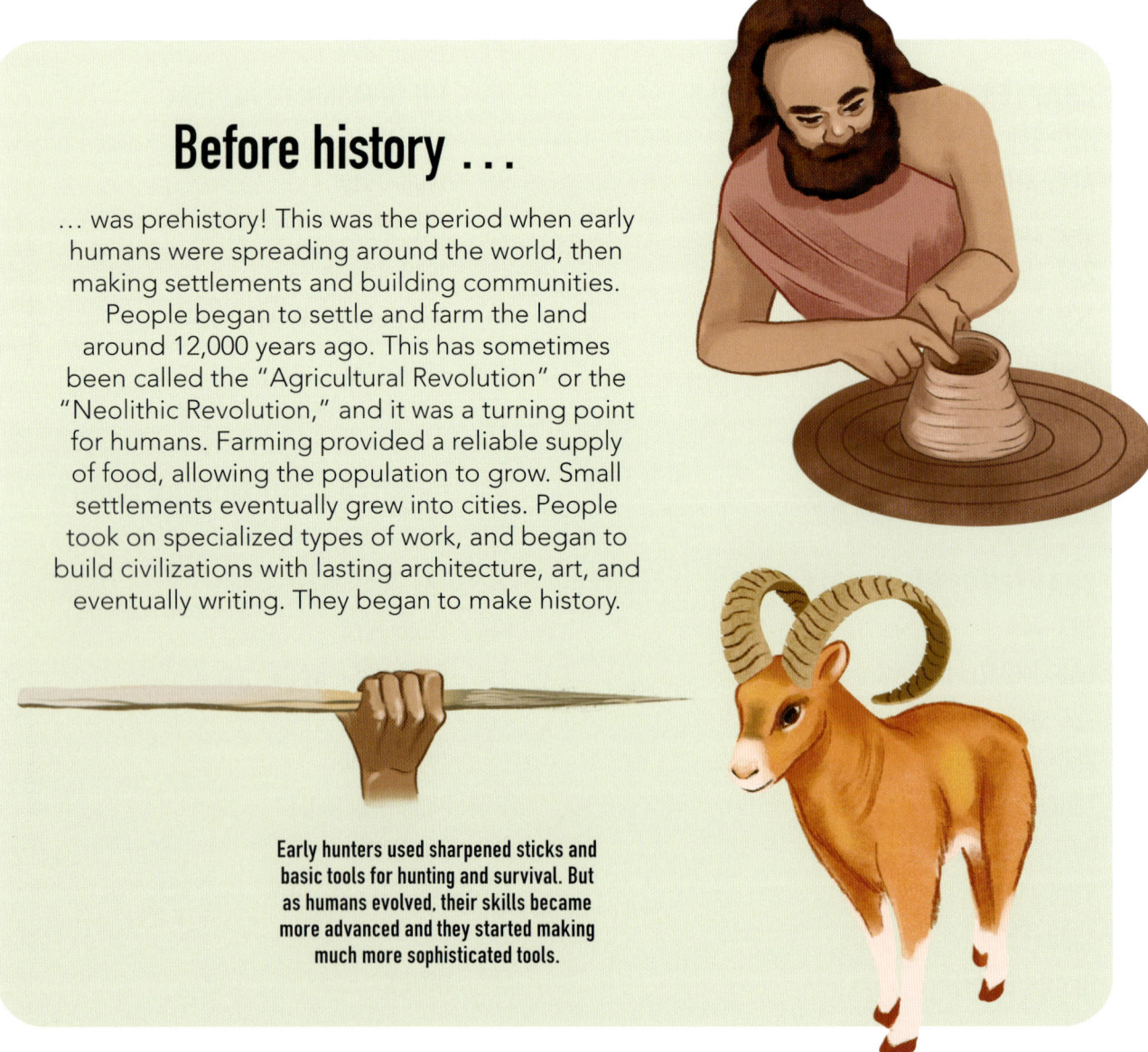

Early hunters used sharpened sticks and basic tools for hunting and survival. But as humans evolved, their skills became more advanced and they started making much more sophisticated tools.

INTRODUCTION

Making history

Many historians think of history as starting around 5,000 years ago (3000 BCE). That's about the time people in some parts of the world developed ways of writing. Although written historical records are very useful to historians, they are not the only kind of historical evidence we can use. We can learn a lot from objects, art, buildings, monuments—and even from graves and dead bodies. History is put together not just by historians, but also archaeologists (who work with buildings and other human-made objects) and anthropologists (who work with evidence of human lives). If we restricted history to only studying written records, we could say nothing at all about cultures that left no writing.

Objects like the Great Sphinx of Giza reveal the skills of people who lived thousands of years ago, but we don't always know how or why they made things like this

Whose history?

When you think of history, you might think of famous individuals, such as rulers or great explorers or scientists. Or you might think of whole cultures that you know something about, such as the Romans, the ancient Chinese, or the Aztecs. You probably don't think of an Australian Indigenous person hunting kangaroo 400 years ago, a Russian serf struggling to survive on frozen farmland in the 18th century, or an Abyssinian woman weaving cloth 3,000 years ago. Most of the people who have ever lived have been ordinary people like this. But without them, the events we do know about could not have happened—they grew the food and made the tools that made everything else possible. Sometimes, we can learn about their lives even if we don't know their names.

We know nothing of the lives of the people who made these vast stone statues in Rapa Nui (Easter Island)

Most people lived ordinary lives that we only know about in general terms

INTRODUCTION

Reading history

We know most about the cultures that have left written records that we can read. Some cultures had writing, but we haven't learned to interpret it yet. Others left no writing at all, and historians can work only from what other cultures have written about them, and from the objects they have left behind.

The Thule of Greenland left no writing, and even the Vikings who encountered them left no accounts of them

Second-hand information

Historians need to be very careful when using what one society has written about another. It's often impossible to say how accurate their accounts are, or whether they had any reason to misrepresent the people they encountered. For example, Europeans often thought of the people already living in lands they wanted to conquer as being unsophisticated, ignorant, or barbaric. They felt this excused them from stealing the land and resources of those people. When one group is at war with another, they frequently present their enemies in a bad light, sometimes making up tales of terrible things they do in order to spur on their own soldiers. It's hard to know, years later, which stories are true.

Viking raids in Europe were recorded by monks, but we don't have the Vikings' own version of what happened

INTRODUCTION

Two sides to history

Even without deliberate bias, there are always at least two sides to any story. The same event reported by two people will sound different, even if they are not opponents. The same event can mean different things to different people.

One thing after another

History is as much about interpreting the events of the past as it is knowing what they were. Events have consequences, and how people feel about events has consequences. Often, it's impossible to see at the time how a situation will work out. But by knowing what has happened in the past, we can try to avoid repeating the same mistakes.

The cotton gin was invented in 1793, to make the work of producing cotton easier. It led to an increase in slavery in the USA, and so indirectly led to the American Civil War.

The random event of the Black Death in the 1340s changed the history of the world

As well as deliberate actions by people, history can be shaped by unexpected events. These range from natural disasters such as an earthquake that destroys a city, to a surprise discovery or invention that forever changes how people live. Fifty years ago, no one could have predicted that we would live much of our lives online. We don't know what will happen next, or which of the things happening now will look most important to future historians, but history is being made all the time.

CHAPTER 1

THE BEGINNING OF HISTORY

The story of world history begins with its prologue—prehistory. This time began when early modern humans spread around the world, starting in Africa, and ventured over land, and eventually sea, to start lives in all kinds of environments. They built homes from the materials available wherever they found themselves, and learned to use fire and make tools and clothes. They finally settled in fixed communities, securing their food supply by keeping animals as livestock and growing plants as crops. This was a time before people had developed written language, so what we know of them and their lives comes from objects they have left behind, including tools, works of art, shelters and other buildings, jewelry, and clothing. Even their bodies provide evidence. We can date bones to discover when people lived in the places where their remains are found, and work out what they ate and even the diseases they suffered from.

Once people began writing, recording the events and experiences of their everyday lives, history began. This started at different times around the world.

— THE BEGINNING OF HISTORY —

PREHISTORY—11,000 YEARS AGO (9000 BCE)

Early modern humans evolved in Africa and first left about 180,000 years ago, spreading into western Asia. Later, waves of migrating people followed. Over thousands of years, they traveled long distances to settle all around the globe. At times, sea levels allowed people to cross land bridges between areas that are now separated by water.

45,000 YEARS AGO
Mammoth-bone shelters were made in Moldova, eastern Europe. The shelters were made from piled mammoth bones covered with hides.

44,000 YEARS AGO
A notched bone and sticks from the Border cave in Africa are the first evidence of humans **counting** or **tallying** (keeping track of numbers).

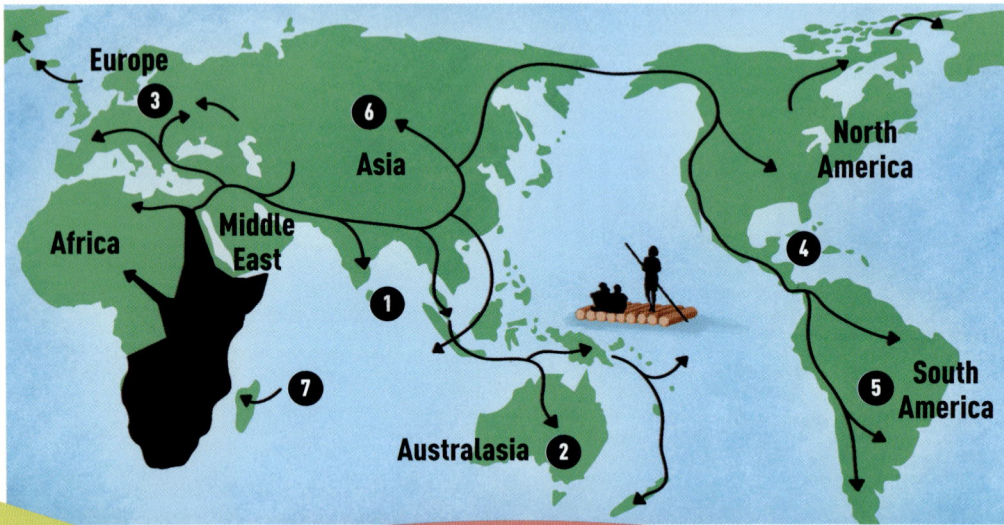

❶ 180,000 years ago
❷ 65,000 years ago
❸ 54,000 years ago
❹ 33,000 years ago
❺ 26,000 years ago
❻ 25,000 years ago
❼ 1,500 years ago

PREHISTORY

110,000–11,700 YEARS AGO
During the last glacial period (or "ice age"), sea levels fell as water was trapped as ice, revealing new **land bridges**. One was Beringia around 35,700 years ago, joining eastern Russia and the west of North America. Another later one (16,000 years ago) was Doggerland, joining Britain to continental Europe.

Ice covered much of North America, northern Russia, and Europe, while land was exposed that is now under water

54,000 YEARS AGO
Early modern humans arrived in **Europe**, joining another type of early human, **Neanderthals**, who already lived there. The two species lived alongside each other and even had families together.

50,000–45,000 YEARS AGO
The first people settled in **Australia**.

45,500 YEARS AGO
People in Indonesia **painted animals** on the walls of their caves.

A cave painting 44,000 years old is the earliest hunting scene

THE BEGINNING OF HISTORY

33,000–30,000 YEARS AGO

The first early humans probably arrived in the **Americas**.

Stone spearheads were fixed to a wooden shaft and used for hunting. Some spearheads were made from mammoth ivory.

c. 30,000 YEARS AGO

The people of Dolní Věstonice in the Czech Republic used a variety of **stone tools** for cutting, hunting, warfare, and piercing holes in leather. They also used **mammoth ivory** to make spearheads—one of the earliest known examples of this type of tool.

Agriculture changed humans, the land, and other species. People bred from the animals that gave the best meat, hide, or milk, reinforcing the characteristics they wanted. They did the same with plants, keeping seed from the best crops to grow the next year. The land was affected by people cutting down trees and clearing scrub to gain farmland, and later by them diverting water to their crops. By living close to each other and their livestock, people also became vulnerable to illness. Diseases moved from animals to people, and spread between those living in close quarters.

12,000 YEARS AGO

There was a shift from migration/hunter-gathering to settled **farming** in communities. This change happened independently at different times globally, with people settling, growing crops, and keeping animals for food. It changed human society forever.

11,000 YEARS AGO (9000 BCE)

12,500 YEARS AGO

Distinctive **"cord marked" pottery** characterized the Jōmon culture of prehistoric Japan.

29,000–15,000 YEARS AGO

Humans began to **domesticate wolves**, using them to guard animals and perhaps communities. Domesticated wolves eventually became dogs.

Wolves were probably domesticated many times, by different groups of people

9600–8200 BCE

The oldest **megaliths** (large stone monuments) were made in Göbekli Tepe, Turkey. Most (95 percent) of the site is still unexplored.

No one knows how the circle of megaliths was used

26,000 YEARS AGO

The people of Dolní Věstonice were already accomplished **artists**, and left behind figures made of ivory and clay.

THE BEGINNING OF HISTORY

8999–3500 BCE

Around 11,700 years ago (9700 BCE), the last glacial period ended. The warmer climate made farming—and life—easier. Settlements grew larger, becoming the first cities. Civilization emerged independently in six places around the world: Egypt, Mesopotamia (now Iraq and Iran), the Indus Valley (now Pakistan and Afghanistan), Mexico, Peru, and China. From here on, dates are given in the form BCE (Before Common Era) and CE (Common Era). The Common Era starts with year 1 in our current date scheme, just over 2,020 years ago. Many dates are approximate.

6000 BCE
The Sahara Desert began to **dry up**, forcing out people who lived there.

8000 BCE
One of the earliest cities, Jericho, was built from **bricks made from clay** baked in the sun.

7000 BCE
People in northeastern Siberia traded in tools made of **obsidian** (volcanic glass), apparently traveling hundreds of miles, probably by dog sled.

6000–4000 BCE
Farmers on the Greek island of Crete grew **olives**, which became a staple of trade.

8999 BCE

8000 BCE
Sea levels rose, separating the islands of Japan from mainland Asia. People who had followed herds overland and started the Jōmon culture in c. 14000 BCE were cut off. As they ran out of animals to eat, they turned to fishing, starting Japan's long tradition of fish-eating.

5000 BCE
In the Atacama desert of Chile and Peru, the Chinchorro people **mummified their dead** 2,000 years before the Egyptians began mummification.

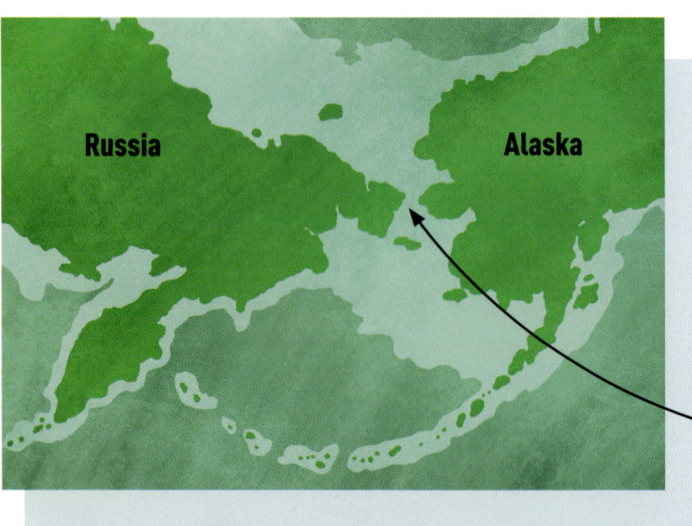

Sea | Land today | Land 10,000 years ago

8000 BCE
Beringia disappeared under the sea. **Warming weather** allowed people to settle in Canada.

With melting ice, sea levels rose, separating Russia and Alaska

Chinchorro bodies were taken apart, dried, then reassembled with padding of soil, ash, and grasses. They were then covered with an ash paste, and painted black.

c. 6000–5000 BCE
In Mesopotamia and elsewhere, oxen were domesticated and **plows** (sometimes spelled "ploughs") for farming were developed.

THE BEGINNING OF HISTORY

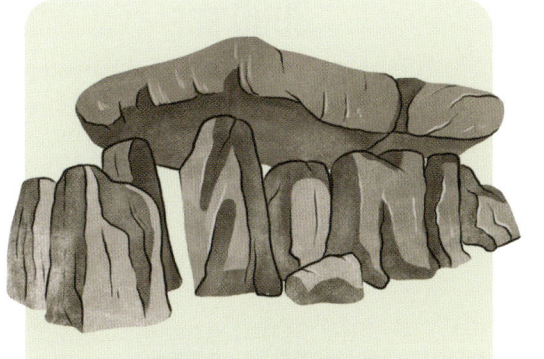

5000–4000 BCE
In France and Britain, people constructed **dolmens** (a stone slab on top of two upright stones) to bury their dead.

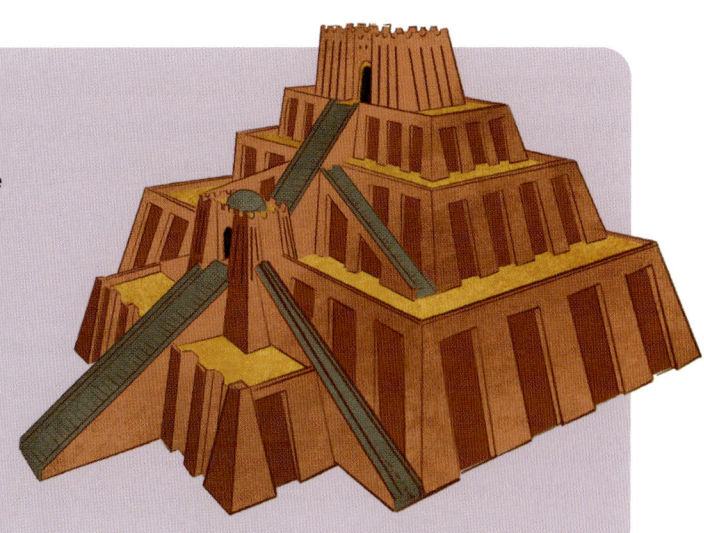

3500 BCE
In Mesopotamia, people built the first **ziggurats** (stepped pyramids) using mud bricks. Considered the earthly homes of gods and goddesses, these were often the first buildings in a new city.

3500 BCE

4000 BCE
Egyptian farmers used tools to break up the soil before **sowing seeds**.

c. 4500 BCE
People in Serbia were the first to **smelt copper** to make tools.

Starting in Serbia around 4500 BCE, people made bronze by mixing tin with copper. From there, the technology gradually spread to other parts of Europe and the Middle East, meaning that the Bronze Age began at different times around the world. It had a huge impact, giving people strong, lasting tools that could be made in complex shapes. This led to the development of more sophisticated agricultural practices, as well as the creation of more effective weapons for hunting and warfare. Those with bronze tools and weapons had a great advantage over groups without them. It also allowed for the creation of more complex societies with greater specialization of labor, and paved the way for further technological advances in metalworking.

3500 BCE–1000 CE
The **Bantu** people spread from the River Niger throughout most of sub-Saharan Africa. They made iron tools, which they used alongside their stone tools. This made their farming efficient. More than 500 modern African languages have developed from Bantu.

3500 BCE
The Telarmachay civilization of the Peruvian Andes kept **llamas and alpacas**, using their hair to make fabrics and eating their meat.

13

THE BEGINNING OF HISTORY

3499–2500 BCE

Larger settlements grew into the first cities. Individuals no longer provided everything needed for themselves and their families. Instead, tasks were shared out—some people grew or prepared food, others built homes, or served the gods. Administration and bureaucracy became essential to organize work and share the benefits.

3000 BCE

The **potter's wheel** was invented as a horizontal surface the potter turned while shaping a pot. The wheel was later adapted for transport.

3490 BCE

On the central Asian steppe, probably in Ukraine or Kazakhstan, people began to **domesticate horses**.

The first domesticated horses were small and stout

3100 BCE

The first **Egyptian dynasty** began, with the unification of southern and northern Egypt. A dynasty is a period when rulers come from the same family line.

3000 BCE

In Mesopotamia, the **shadoof** was used to lift water in a bucket from a river, pool, or well. A heavy counterweight lifted the filled bucket. With a shadoof, people could water their crops more easily, since the work of lifting was done by the lever, not the farmworker.

3499 BCE

3100–2800 BCE

Sumer (in modern Iraq) rose in power. It remained one of the most important regions for thousands of years.

The Indus Valley civilization in Pakistan, Afghanistan, and India began around 3300 BCE. An extremely sophisticated civilization, it had advanced building and town planning, with good plumbing (including flushing toilets) and roads set out on a grid pattern. The largest cities, Harappa and Mohenjo-daro, had up to 50,000 people, when most large cities elsewhere had only 10,000. Oddly, there were no temples or palaces. Little is known about the Indus Valley's history.

Skara Brae homes had turf roofs

3100–2500 BCE

Homes in **Skara Brae**, Scotland, were made from stone layered with earth. Their furniture was also made of stone.

3000–1700 BCE

The **Longshan culture** flourished around the Yellow River in China, where the fertile soil made crops productive. It's famous for its highly polished black pottery. A surviving platform for observing the Sun shows us that the Longshan studied astronomy.

3000–1100 BCE

The Minoans on Crete were the first **European civilization**. They made maze-like palaces, fine jewelry and pottery, and vivid frescoes showing daily life.

THE BEGINNING OF HISTORY

2670 BCE
The **step pyramid of Djoser** was the first Egyptian pyramid. At 62 m (204 ft) tall, it was the highest structure of its time.

The Djoser pyramid was built by piling up massive stone blocks

2550 BCE
The stones were put in place at **Stonehenge**, in southern England, although the site was probably in use from 3100 BCE. The entrance to the central circle lined up with sunrise at midsummer and sunset at midwinter.

Massive stones weighing up to 4,000 kg (9,000 lb) were hauled 300 km (185 miles) to make Stonehenge

2613–2181 BCE
In the "Old Kingdom" of Ancient Egypt, most kings demanded vast **pyramids** as memorial tombs. These took huge amounts of work and materials to build.

2500 BCE

c. 2500–350 BCE
The Kingdom of Kush in Nubia (now Sudan and Egypt) developed an advanced civilization in which **women played a more prominent role** than elsewhere in the ancient world.

2558–2532 BCE
The mysterious **Great Sphinx of Giza**, located in Egypt, was probably carved during the reign of Khafre, but might be older. No one knows its purpose. It was the largest statue in the world.

The Great Sphinx is 73 m (240 ft) long and 20 m (66 ft) high

2500 BCE
Ancient Egyptians began to **mummify their dead**. They removed the internal organs and used preservative chemicals, before wrapping the body in linen bandages.

A painted mask often covered the face of an Egyptian mummy

THE BEGINNING OF HISTORY

THE START OF HISTORY

History begins with the written record of events. Writing developed independently in several cultures around the world, and we know most about those cultures that left writing we can read. That doesn't mean that cultures without writing, or whose writing we can't yet decipher, knew less or were less sophisticated or advanced—we simply know less about them.

THE FERTILE CRESCENT

The "Fertile Crescent" is the area around the rivers Tigris, Euphrates, and Nile that was home to the Mesopotamian and Egyptian civilizations. The first writing developed here around 3400–3300 BCE. In Mesopotamia (in Iraq), people used a stick called a **stylus** to press wedge-shaped marks into soft clay **tablets**. The tablets were then baked to harden them. Many thousands of clay tablets have survived. This type of writing is called **cuneiform**. It used symbols to represent the sounds that make up words. The Sumerians used cuneiform for official documents and accounts, but also for poetry, medical texts, astronomical accounts, and records of events.

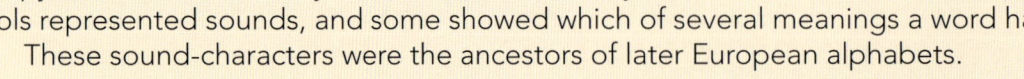

Soon after, around 3250–3200 BCE, Egyptian scribes began using a type of picture writing. Symbols began as recognizable images of objects, such as a foot, a bowl, or an eagle. They were called **hieroglyphs** when carved in stone, and **hieratic** when written with reed pens or brushes on papyrus. Over time, the symbols became more stylized. Some symbols represented sounds, and some showed which of several meanings a word had. These sound-characters were the ancestors of later European alphabets.

THE BEGINNING OF HISTORY

AROUND THE WORLD

Mesopotamia and Egypt were close together, and writing in one place perhaps influenced its development nearby. People in **China** developed writing independently with no clear path to join them to the Fertile Crescent. The people of **Mesoamerica** made their own writing systems around 900–600 BCE with no link to Europe, Asia, or Africa. The Chinese character system was pictographic, again starting with pictures that later became less recognizable. The earliest Chinese characters are inscribed on "oracle bones"—shards of bone or tortoise shell used to try to predict what the future might bring. China had a fully functional writing system by 1300 BCE.

The early character for mountains (top) looks like a mountain range, but the modern character (bottom) is more stylized

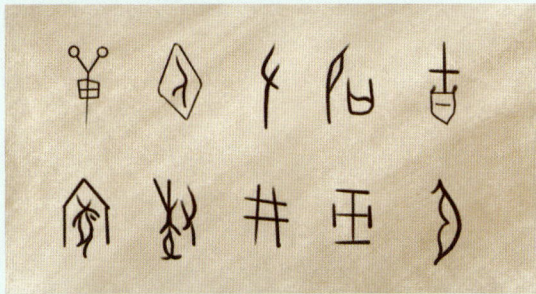

Chinese characters from oracle bones, around 1500 BCE

GLYPHS AND STRINGS

In Mesoamerica (from Mexico to Costa Rica), the Mayans used **glyphs** painted onto codices (books) made of deer skin or tree bark, or carved into stone. Few of these books survive, as many were destroyed by European invaders in the 1500s. One unique way of recording numbers, and possibly also words, was the **quipu** made of knotted strings hanging from a backbone string. The quipu code has not yet been interpreted.

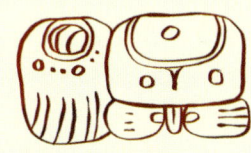

Quipu

Glyphs (above) were made by putting different components together. The three components of this glyph (top) are shown by the blue, green, and yellow drawings underneath it.

MYSTERIES REMAIN

The **Indus Valley** civilization left many stone seals, but these have not been decoded. There are only 400 known characters, which is too few for a system that uses a different symbol for each word. Wooden tablets from **Rapa Nui** (Easter Island), called "rongorongo" use 120 glyphs to produce texts up to 2,320 characters long, but their meaning has been lost. Writing might have emerged independently here, too.

A stone seal from the Indus Valley, around 2000 BCE

THE BEGINNING OF HISTORY

2499–1500 BCE

Some cities grew, taking over surrounding land and settlements, and becoming kingdoms and empires. But large communities were vulnerable to disasters such as floods, failing crops, disease, and attack from others. Some cities and kingdoms fell. Those that survived produced the first literature and astronomy, and some important inventions that made these civilizations even more successful.

2000 BCE
The Indus Valley civilization **tamed elephants**. They used them for forestry work, in wars, and in ceremonies.

2000 BCE
The last **woolly mammoths died** on Wrangel Island, which is located in the Arctic Ocean. The iconic ice age mammals that lived in the unique environment on the island had survived thousands of years longer than those on the mainland, but eventually they too died out, due to a combination of different factors.

2334–2279 BCE
Sargon of Akkad created the first empire in **Mesopotamia**, bringing together several kingdoms. Efficient and widespread administration helped it succeed.

c. 2030 BCE
The earliest **code of laws**, the Code of Ur-Nammu, was produced in Sumer. Some crimes were punishable by death, but most brought only a fine.

2499 BCE

2285–2250 BCE
The first known named **author**, the Mesopotamian poet Enheduanna, was probably the daughter of Sargon of Akkad.

2180 BCE
The **Old Kingdom in Egypt collapsed**. Civil war, drought, and famine ravaged the land until the Middle Kingdom was founded in 2040 BCE.

2150–1400 BCE
Gilgamesh was written—the oldest epic in world literature. It tells of Gilgamesh's journey to seek eternal life after the death of his friend.

1900–1500 BCE
The **Indus Valley civilization declined**, perhaps because of climate change, the drying of the Sarasvati River, and falling trade with Egypt.

THE BEGINNING OF HISTORY

1800 BCE
The Mesopotamian army used **war chariots**, allowing soldiers to shoot arrows at enemies while moving. Horse-drawn chariots were used from around 2000 BCE in the Steppe, before people began to ride on horseback.

c. 1750–1500 BCE
Assyrian astronomers in northern Mesopotamia identified the **five planets** readily visible to the naked eye: Mercury, Venus, Mars, Jupiter, and Saturn. Some of the names they gave to constellations of stars are still used today.

The Olmec made giant stone heads

1500–200 BCE
The **Olmec civilization**, in the Gulf of Mexico, built great cities of stone and brick. They were the first culture in South America.

1500 BCE

1795–1750 BCE
The Babylonian **Code of Hammurabi** set out punishments for a wide range of crimes, demanding like-for-like physical penalties such as "an eye for an eye."

1700–1100 BCE
Indigenous Americans made **Poverty Point**, a huge system of earthworks, with a large mound and concentric semicircles.

c. 1600 BCE
The first historical Chinese dynasty, the **Shang**, began.

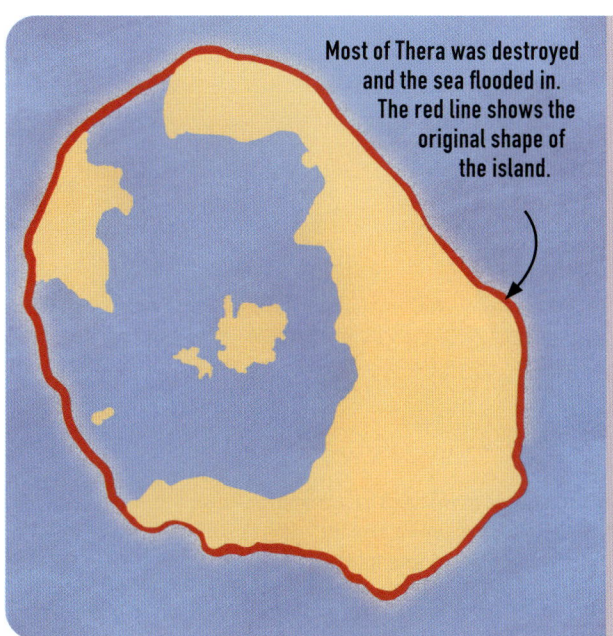

Most of Thera was destroyed and the sea flooded in. The red line shows the original shape of the island.

c. 1650–1550 BCE
A **volcano** on the Greek island of **Thera** (Santorini) erupted catastrophically, blowing the island apart. Earthquakes, giant waves, and a thick blanket of ash destroyed settlements in nearby lands. It was the most powerful eruption of the last 10,000 years.

1500 BCE
People in South America first domesticated and grew **cocoa beans**.

1500 BCE
The first writings in Sanskrit, the Vedas, laid down the basics of the **Hindu religion**. The Indian caste system began at this time, dividing people into different social levels depending on the type of work did, and dictating what they were allowed to do.

THE BEGINNING OF HISTORY

CHINESE DYNASTIES

A dynasty is a ruling family that passes down leadership from one generation to the next. Dynasties have been common around the world, from the Egyptian pharaohs to European royal families, but perhaps the most famous are those from China. The history of China is traditionally divided into dynasties, with the start of a new dynasty beginning a new chapter in the history of the land.

GETTING STARTED

The first Chinese dynasty, the **Xia**, is considered mythical by many historians. It supposedly started with Yu the Great around 2100 BCE and lasted until around 1600 BCE, when the first dynasty that has been historically verified began. Yu is said to have made China stable and wealthy by controlling flood waters with irrigation channels.

The first historical dynasty, the **Shang**, started after the Shang leader Tang overthrew the tyrant Jie. The Shang created a stable government and encouraged many advances, including a standardized writing system, industrial casting of bronze, a 365-day calendar, and religious rituals. The Shang dynasty ended in 1046 BCE when the emperor **Zhou**, who had become a lazy, self-indulgent tyrant, was overthrown by King Wu of the province Zhou.

The legendary Yu the Great

CHANGING HANDS

Chinese rulers claimed to rule by virtue of the **Mandate of Heaven**, beginning with the Zhou dynasty. Supposedly, the heavens chose a just ruler and supported him, so to overthrow him would mean defying the heavens. But if the heavens were displeased with a ruler, terrible things could happen, such as earthquakes, famines, and rebellions. These were taken as signs that the emperor had lost the mandate of heaven and a new ruler should be chosen, starting another dynasty. The system made **astrology** very important to the Chinese, as events in the heavens were thought to have an impact on events on Earth.

An unexpected event, such as a comet, could be taken as a bad omen—a sign the heavens were displeased with an emperor

THE BEGINNING OF HISTORY

WRITING IT DOWN

Oracle bone script

We know about the Shang dynasty because the first Chinese writing comes from this time, inscribed on **oracle bones**. Priests scratched questions into the bones, then heated them to make them crack. From the pattern of cracks, they tried to work out the gods' answers to the questions. Objects and writings from a historic time are valuable to historians as "primary sources"—direct evidence of what happened.

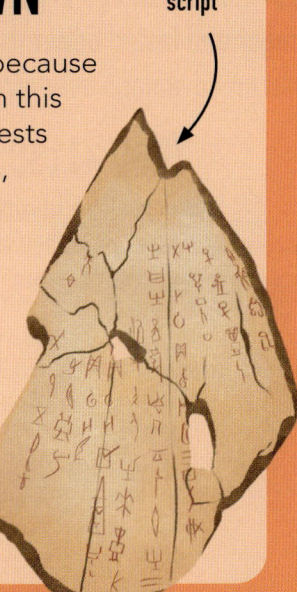

BETWEEN DYNASTIES

Early dynastic rule wasn't stable. China covers a large area, and it was impossible for a leader to keep control of it all the time. In the **Spring and Autumn Period** of 770–475 BCE and the following **Warring States Period**, many local leaders began fighting between themselves. At times, there were over 1,000 small states; by the end of the Warring States Period, warlords had gathered these together into seven major states at war with each other.

CHINA UNITED

The extent of the Chinese state under the Xia, Zhou, and Qin dynasties

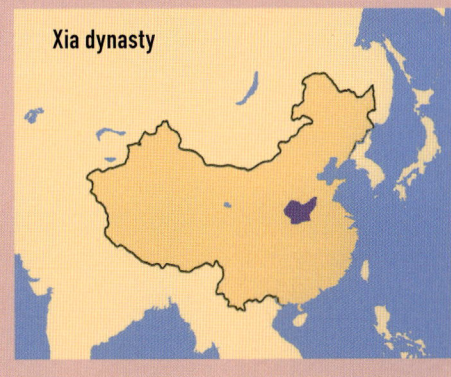
Xia dynasty

The seven states were eventually brought under the control of a single ruler—Shi Huangdi, who became the first **Qin** emperor in 221 BCE. In 230 BCE, the Han state surrendered to Qin, afraid of attack. The next state, Wei, surrendered after Shi diverted a river to flood the main city, causing devastation. Shi quickly took over the remaining states. He united China and held it together by a mix of military force, moving all power to the central administration, and removing borders between states. The name "China" comes from "Qin" (pronounced "chin").

Although Shi's rule was short (he died in 210 BCE), the united imperial China he built remained until the end of the last dynasty, the Qing, in 1912.

Zhou dynasty

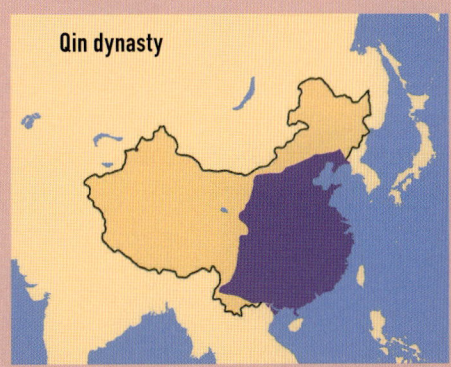
Qin dynasty

■ Extent under the named dynasty
■ Extent of modern China

THE BEGINNING OF HISTORY

1499–800 BCE

A period known as the "Bronze Age Collapse" saw the end of the Bronze Age in Europe and the start of the Iron Age. Iron tools and weapons were stronger and lasted better than their bronze counterparts, and people who gained them early had an advantage over rivals.

c. 1490 BCE
The **Phoenician civilization** grew from city-states along the Mediterranean coast of Syria, Lebanon, and northern Israel. The Phoenicians were a sea-based, trading culture. The Greek alphabet and mythology probably had their origins in Phoenicia.

1450 BCE
All the palaces of the Minoan civilization of Crete were destroyed by fire, except Knossos. The fires were probably started by **Mycenaean invaders**. The Mycenae spread from southern Greece and into nearby lands, including Cyprus, the Levant, and Egypt.

1250–1150 BCE
Bronze Age civilizations around the Mediterranean **collapsed**. Cities were destroyed, writing systems disappeared, trade stopped, and there was widespread death. Earthquakes, climate change, famine, rebellions, and invasions have all been suggested as causes. The Bronze Age was followed by the Iron Age.

1208–1176 BCE
Attacks by the **Sea Peoples** destroyed (or helped to destroy) the civilizations of the Mycenae in Greece and the Hittites in Anatolia, Turkey, but their attacks on Egypt failed. The Sea Peoples were groups of migrants and refugees from Central Europe. People from areas they attacked probably also became refugees, increasing the chaos.

1499 BCE

1258 BCE
Egyptian pharaoh Rameses II made peace with invading Hittites, from Turkey, recorded in one of the oldest surviving **peace treaties**.

1100 BCE
The Lapita, ancestors of Polynesian navigators, settled in **Fiji**, having crossed the ocean in small wooden boats.

1324 BCE
Tutankhamen, king of Egypt, died at the age of 19 and was buried in a splendid tomb in the Valley of the Kings. The discovery of his tomb in 1922 revealed much about Ancient Egypt.

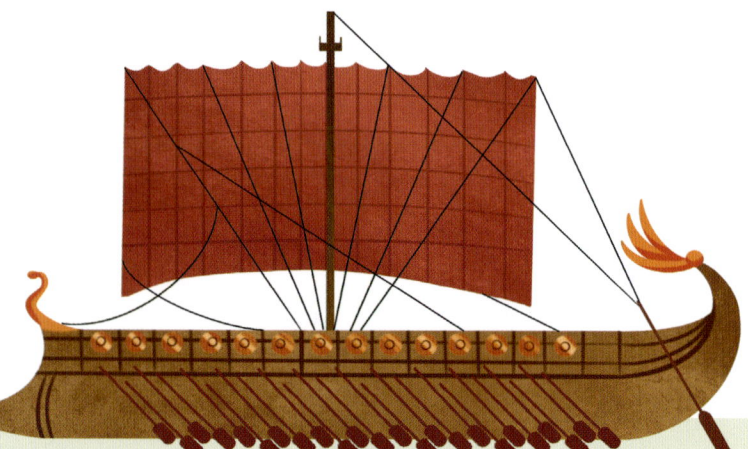

1100 BCE
Phoenician ship-builders developed the **war galley**. Driven by both oars and wind, it was fitted with a battering ram at the front which could smash into enemy ships.

THE BEGINNING OF HISTORY

1100–900 BCE
The **Lapita people** set out from Taiwan to settle the far-flung islands of the Pacific Ocean.

900–600 BCE
The **Assyrian Empire** became one of the first world empires, controlling land now in parts of Iran, Kuwait, Syria, and Turkey. It rose to power through war, using iron weapons. The Assyrian army was the first to have an engineering department setting up ladders and ramps, filling in moats, and digging trenches.

930–900 BCE
People used **domesticated camels** in Israel to move products made by the copper-smelting industry.

800 BCE

1046 BCE
The **Zhou dynasty** replaced the Shang dynasty in China, claiming the "Mandate of Heaven" to support their rule.

10TH CENTURY BCE
King Solomon is said to have built the **first temple in Jerusalem**. No evidence of the temple exists, and it's impossible to excavate the city to look for it.

1000 BCE
Steppe nomads, particularly those of Central Asia, perfected the use of the bow and arrow from horseback, becoming the first **cavalry** units in history. They became skilled archers, capable of shooting accurately while riding at full gallop. This hit-and-run style of warfare, known as horse archery, gave them a big advantage, as it was very effective at causing confusion among infantry units and disrupting enemy formations.

800 BCE
The early Dorset people moved into western **Greenland** from Canada, taking over from the Saqqaq, who had lived across Greenland from around 2500 BCE.

THE BEGINNING OF HISTORY

799–500 BCE

In Europe, the rise of Ancient Greece began, and the first civilization appeared in Italy. In Greece, the first evidence of a scientific approach to understanding the world, and the first steps toward democracy, laid the foundations of the modern world.

705–681 BCE
The Assyrian king Sennacherib systematically **sacked** the city of **Babylon** in Mesopotamia.

6TH CENTURY BCE
The first known **gold coins** were struck in Lydia, an area of modern Turkey, probably before 546 BCE.

776 BCE
The first **Olympic Games** were held in Greece, and then every four years for more than 1,000 years. The first 12 Games had only one contest, a running race.

650 BCE
Crossbows were used in China. Less physical strength is needed to use a crossbow than a traditional bow.

c. 594 BCE
In Athens, Greece, the lawmaker Solon divided the citizens into four groups, allowing them varying degrees of involvement in **running the city**. It was a move away from one ruling class making all the decisions.

799 BCE

753 BCE
According to legend, **Rome** was founded by Romulus. Romulus and Remus were supposedly twin sons of the god Mars, abandoned at birth and suckled by a wolf. When they grew up, they fought over where to build a city, Romulus killing Remus.

600 BCE
Celtic artists developed the motif of the long, stringy **ribbon monster** that often bites its own tail, or that of another monster.

585 BCE
The Greek-Turkish philosopher **Thales of Miletus** reportedly predicted a solar eclipse. He's considered the first person to take a scientific approach to the skies, trying to explain how the universe works in terms of physical causes and effects, without relying on gods.

750 BCE
The **Etruscan civilization** appeared as city-states in northern and western Italy.

THE BEGINNING OF HISTORY

575 BCE
King Nebuchadnezzar II built the **Ishtar Gate** at one of the entrances to the city of Babylon. It was one of the most famous and beautiful constructions of the ancient world.

c. 551–479 BCE
The Chinese philosopher **Confucius** taught the importance of living a virtuous life, and of respect for one's ancestors. He believed rulers should be kind and not extravagant, and that inner peace was linked to balance in the outer world.

550 BCE
Cyrus the Great began building the first **Persian Empire**, invading and conquering Lydia (an area of modern Turkey), Armenia, and Babylon.

6TH–5TH CENTURY BCE
The Romans developed their system of **numerals**.

509 BCE
The last of the Roman kings was overthrown, establishing the **Roman Republic**.

500 BCE

508 BCE
The Athenian statesman Cleisthenes **reorganized Athens**, dividing the (male) population into 139 "demes." Men registered in a deme could take part in political decision-making.

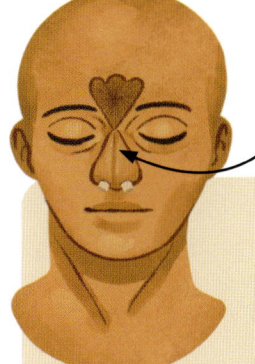

Skin flap folded over to make a new nose

550 BCE
Surgeons in India carried out **plastic surgery**, reconstructing noses for those who had lost theirs as a punishment or in battle. A flap of skin was lifted from the forehead and twisted around to form a new nose. Straws kept the nostrils open while the nose healed.

Darius I (Darius the Great) became king of Persia in 522 BCE. He greatly extended the empire, including parts of India, Egypt, Greece, and Europe. He started grand building projects, reformed the laws, standardized weights and measures, and introduced a new currency. His laws still form the basis of Iranian law. Darius started the Greco-Persian wars in 499 BCE, which continued until 449 BCE. He died in 486 BCE, and was succeeded by his eldest son Xerxes.

505 BCE
The city-states of northern Greece united under the largest state, Sparta, forming the **Peloponnesian League**.

THE BEGINNING OF HISTORY

FORMS OF GOVERNMENT

We know little about how the earliest social groups were organized, but from the start of history, it seems that most cultures had a chieftain or king in charge. We would now call this system a monarchy. As civilizations grew larger and more complex, they needed more complicated forms of civic organization and more bureaucracy (rules, staff, and systems) to keep them running.

HUNTING, GATHERING, AND MOVING

Before the start of farming, people lived in small groups of to up to 100 individuals. They moved around the land, hunting animals and collecting roots, fruit, nuts, and seeds to eat. Cooperation was important, but little formal organization was needed. **Hunter-gatherer communities** continued in some places until around 1500 CE, but few survive now. One existing group is the Hadza in Tanzania. The social structure of the Hadza people includes different "bands" that have no hierarchy (tiers of authority or wealth). Instead, decisions are reached communally by discussion. Earlier hunter-gatherers perhaps lived in a similar way.

SETTLED AND STRUCTURED

Larger, settled groups needed much more organization than a hunter-gatherer tribe. When each person was no longer searching for their own food and making their own weapons and tools, society needed a structure that would **share out work and property**.

A VOICE OF AUTHORITY

Larger communities often developed a **hierarchy**, with one person or group having more wealth and power than others. At first, it might have been the person who was physically stronger or could gather more supporters who took charge. This **chieftain** or **monarch** then had the authority to organize the society in a way that kept them in power. They were often in danger of being overthrown, either by someone within the group, or by outsiders. The role of chief or monarch was often hereditary, and passed down a family line. The remains of many early settlements include palaces that apparently belonged to a leader. Even when there are no written records to tell us how a community was run, grand buildings and fine objects suggest someone was monarch.

Statue of an early South American chieftain, 300–600 CE

THE BEGINNING OF HISTORY

KINGS, GODS, AND EMPERORS

In some places, kings claimed the authority of a **god** to support their rule. In ancient Egypt, part of the pharaoh's role was to attend religious ceremonies, keeping peace with the gods. As a civic leader, the pharaoh made laws, decided when the country should go to war, and collected taxes to pay for public goods.

Some rulers even claimed to be directly descended from gods. This made it difficult for rivals to challenge their position. If the emperor had divine approval or was a god, rebelling against him became spiritually, as well as physically, dangerous. The emperors of Japan claimed descent from the sun god.

BY THE PEOPLE, FOR THE PEOPLE

A new approach to government began in ancient Athens at the end of the 6th century BCE. It was the start of **democracy**—a form of government in which the people either make political decisions themselves, as a group, or they elect representatives to make decisions for them. This saw a move away from rule by a very small group (such as a royal family or the very wealthy) to rule by public consent. Athenian democracy was not like modern democracy, as only free men (not slaves or women) were allowed to vote.

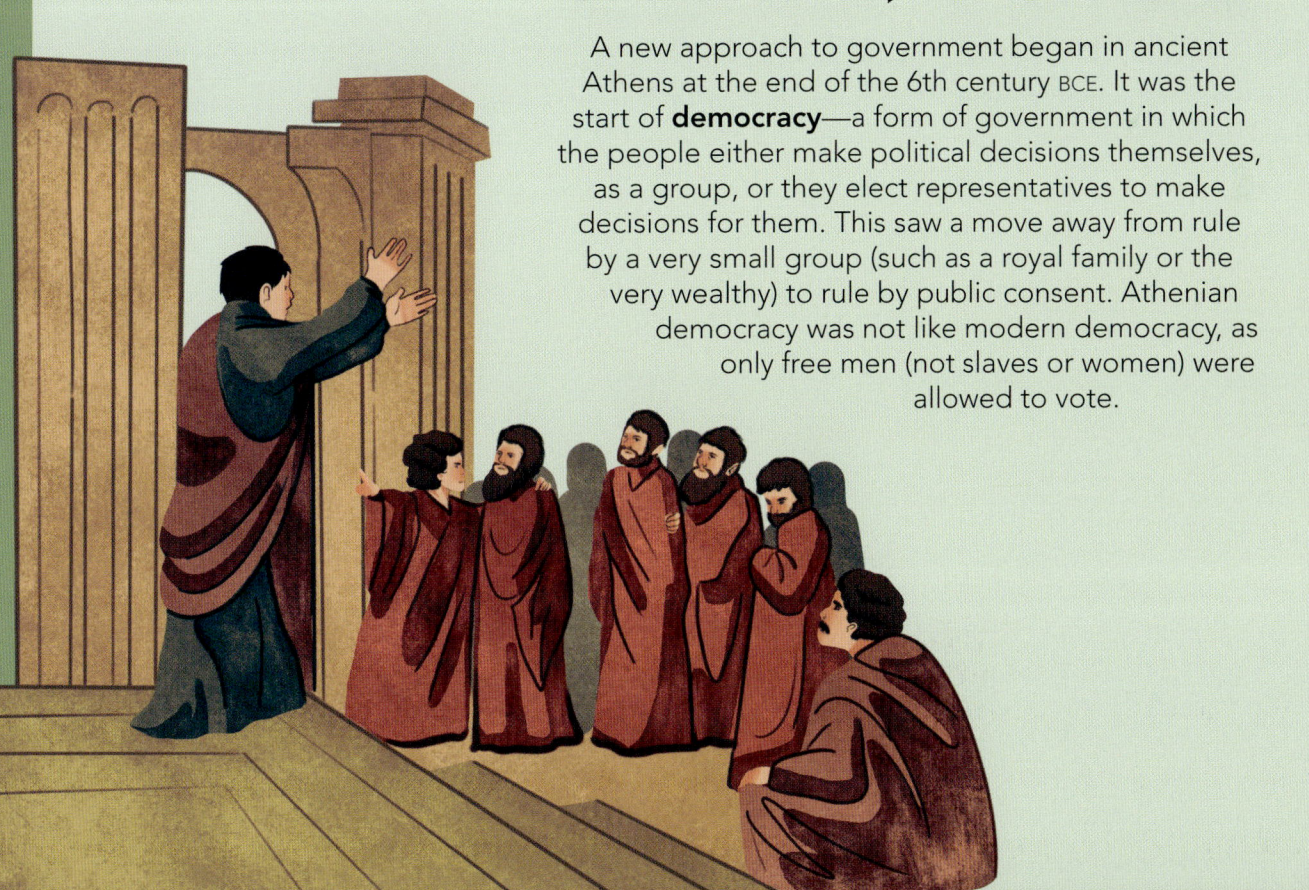

CHAPTER 2

THE ANCIENT WORLD

The 1,000 years around the start of the Common Era (CE) saw huge changes around the world. It was a time of mighty empires rising and falling. It also saw the great religions of the world coming into place—and sometimes pitting themselves against each other.

We have detailed histories of the events, wars, and campaigns of the Mediterranean and Middle Eastern powers, of China, and North Africa. We know the names of important figures in these regions, and sometimes we have several accounts of events left by different groups. This is especially useful to historians, as different accounts of events rarely agree fully. Historians look for evidence of what happened and why—yet the accounts are often biased toward showing an individual's or group's own actions in a good light. Having more than one account, particularly from opposing sides of battles and disputes, helps historians to build a fuller picture.

Some parts of the world, though, still left few or no written records, and we know less of what happened there. For instance, we don't know about the events that shaped some of the cultures of North and South America, Australasia, Russia, the Arctic, and much of Africa.

THE ANCIENT WORLD

499–350 BCE

In Europe, the Greeks were the leading civilization. The greatest works of Greek philosophy, science, and literature date from the 5th and 4th centuries BCE. But it was also a time of war and unrest.

480 BCE
The **Han Gou Canal** in China was built, linking the Yangtze River to the Huai River. This, and other ancient canals, became the basis for the Grand Canal that was completed about a century later and still exists today.

5TH CENTURY BCE
In China, Sun Tzu wrote **The Art of War**, giving strategies for military operations, including the value of espionage (spying). The book is still influential today.

The original *Art of War* was written on slats of bamboo that were tied together

499 BCE

490 BCE
Under Darius I, the Persian army attacked Athens. The Greeks defeated them with a much smaller, but better-equipped army at the **Battle of Marathon**.

481–221 BCE
The **Warring States Period** in China saw vicious battles between rival states, each trying to gain land and power. Yet China made great advances in agriculture, trade, philosophy, and the arts in this time.

480 BCE
Darius's successor, Xerxes I, attacked the Greek city-states led by **Sparta**. The Greeks defeated the invaders. The wars ended with a peace treaty in 449 BCE.

450–325 BCE
In Mexico, the **Olmec culture declined** and abandoned the city of La Venta.

Ancient Greece was divided into over 1,000 "city-states," which were politically independent regions. Many consisted of a walled city and surrounding countryside. They were differently governed. For example, Sparta had two kings, but Athens was a democracy.

431–404 BCE
The Spartans and Athenians fought the **Peloponnesian War**. The defeat of Athens saw the end of the "golden age" of Ancient Greece.

A modern marathon race roughly matches the distance from Marathon to Athens, said to have been run by a messenger bringing news of the Athenian victory

THE ANCIENT WORLD

5TH CENTURY BCE
Jewish scribes wrote the **Torah** sometime in the 6th or 5th centuries BCE. It describes the origin of the Jewish people and of the world. According to tradition, the words were given divinely to Moses in 1312 BCE.

390–387 BCE
In western Europe, Celtic tribes under **Brennus** successfully attacked Roman soldiers outside Rome. The Celts raided the undefended city, and eventually agreed to peace in exchange for gold.

430–427 BCE
The **Plague of Athens** killed around a third of the population of the city, or 75,000–100,000 people. It's not certain which disease the plague was.

350 BCE

c. 416 BCE
The statesman Pericles comes to power in Athens and begins to introduce reforms to the city-state's government that become the basis of modern **democracy**.

5TH CENTURY BCE
In India, Siddhartha Gautama left his home sometime beween the 6th and 4th centuries BCE to wander, begging and meditating. After being enlightened while meditating under a tree, he became the **Buddha**.

The Paracas culture flourished for several hundred years in Peru around 800 BCE. It was known for brightly patterned textiles of cotton and alpaca or llama wool, and a necropolis (a complex of tombs). In the 5th to 3rd centuries BCE, mummies were wrapped in splendid woven and embroidered cloths.

Paracas textile from the 5th–3rd century BCE

THE ANCIENT WORLD

ALEXANDER THE GREAT

One of the most important figures of the late centuries BCE was Alexander the Great. A military leader from Macedonia, Greece, he built a vast empire, and spread Greek culture as far as India.

FATHER OF A CONQUEROR

Philip II of Macedon, Alexander's father, became king of Macedonia in 359 BCE. He **reformed the army** to march in closely packed rectangular blocks (phalanxes) of foot soldiers armed with spears and protected with shields. This strategy made them hard to defeat, and he conquered most of Greece. He planned to invade the Persian Empire but was murdered in 336 BCE.

As a young man, Philip II of Macedon lost his right eye in battle

CONQUERING HERO

Alexander (356–323 BCE) was only 20 years old when he took over his father's kingdom in 336 BCE. Following his father's plan to conquer the Persian Empire, he led his army through Egypt, Syria, and Iraq, without ever suffering defeat. At the age of just 25, after a glorious victory at the Battle of Gaugamela (336 BCE), he was king of Greece, ruler of Asia Minor, pharaoh of Egypt, and king of Persia. He marched farther east, building an empire that stretched from the River Danube in Europe to the River Ganges in India. His military expeditions were bold, and he won against almost impossible odds. Finally, in India, his troops would go no farther, wanting to return home. Alexander died of fever in Babylon at the age of 33. By then, he had built the **greatest empire the world had ever seen**.

The dark red area shows the extent of Alexander's empire

THE ANCIENT WORLD

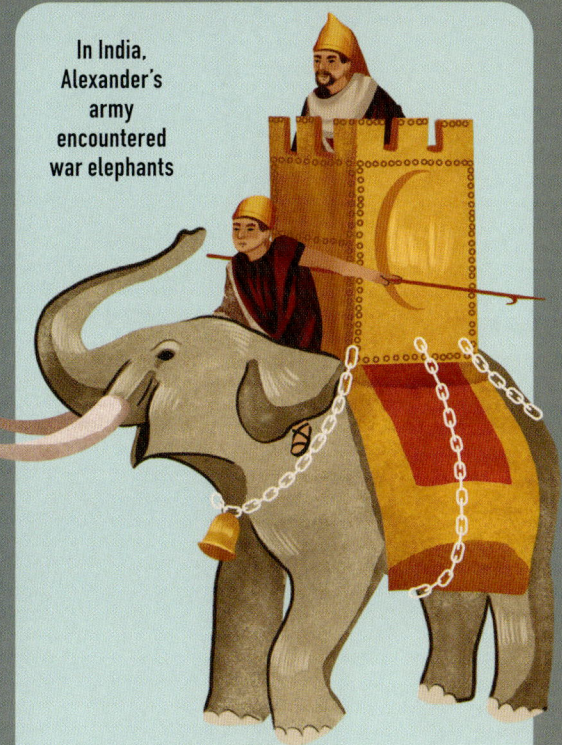

In India, Alexander's army encountered war elephants

Alexander named a city after his beloved warhorse, Bucephalus

NEW WORLDS

Alexander was more than just a brilliant soldier. The Greek philosopher Aristotle had been his personal tutor, and Alexander grew into a **cultured and curious man**. He took scientists to the lands he conquered to investigate the new plants, animals, and geology. He brought cultures together, spreading Greek learning and practices, but also adapting to and respecting local practices. In Egypt, he restored Egyptian temples and made offerings to the gods at Memphis; in Persia, he adopted elements of court dress and customs. But he was principally a conqueror. His army slaughtered defeated soldiers and sold women and children as slaves. He allowed the great Persian city Persepolis to burn, and destroyed and looted many other great cities.

CULTURE WARS

War often causes only destruction, but Alexander built many cities in the lands he took. One of the first and greatest was **Alexandria** in Egypt. It became the capital of Egypt. By spreading Greek culture and language widely, Alexander began the age of Hellenistic (Greek) Egypt. For 300 years, areas of the Middle East used the Greek language and continued to develop Greek culture, now combined with that of Egypt, Persia, and Mesopotamia. This rich cross-fertilization laid the foundations for the intellectual development of Europe, North Africa and the Near East over the next 2,000 years. When Alexander died in 323 BCE, the empire soon broke up, with fighting over it continuing for 40 years.

The amphitheater at Ai-Khanoum, on the borders of Russia and Afghanistan, is an example of Greek architecture far from Greece

THE ANCIENT WORLD

349–250 BCE

While Alexander the Great was conquering half the then-known world, other empires were growing. In India and Egypt, rulers tightened their grips and extended their lands. The world was opening up, too, with sea routes starting to be developed between the Mediterranean Sea and China. Most sailors still followed the coastline, even 1,000 years after the Lapita sailed the Pacific.

338 BCE
Philip II of Macedon took control of most of Greece.

c. 300 BCE
Brahma (the creator), Vishnu (the preserver), and Shiva (the destroyer) emerged as the three main gods in the Vedic religion of India, which became **Hinduism**. These gods were believed to regulate the world, although Hinduism has many additional gods.

Shiva

Brahma

Vishnu

349 BCE

336 BCE
Alexander the Great took over as king of Macedonia. One of the greatest military leaders the world has ever seen, he conquered land over three continents: Europe, Africa, and Asia.

323 BCE
Alexander the Great died in Babylon.

305/4 BCE
Originally a general in Alexander the Great's army, Ptolemy claimed Egypt in the division of the empire after Alexander's death, founding the **Ptolemaic dynasty** that lasted until 30 BCE. He made Alexandria the capital, and had the greatest library of the ancient world built there.

From 300 CE
The Romans built about 80,000 km (50,000 miles) of stone roads to link the various parts of their empire, and make the movement of armies, people, and goods easier. These roads, known as "Viae Romanae," had curved surfaces, so that water drained to the sides. They also had ditches, bridleways, and footpaths alongside. Many of these roads can still be traced, or else have been incorporated into modern road systems in parts of Europe.

321 BCE
Chandragupta Maurya, helped by statesman and philosopher Kautilya, established the first Indian empire. The reputation of Chandragupta's great and powerful army perhaps led to Alexander the Great's troops refusing to go farther into India. Chandragupta ruled for 24 years, his empire covering all of India, except the very south and the extreme northeast.

THE ANCIENT WORLD

3RD CENTURY BCE
The Berbers of North Africa established two **Libyan kingdoms**, Numidia and Mauretania.

264 BCE
The first **gladiatorial contests** took place in Rome. Gladiators trained to fight in an arena as a form of public entertainment. They fought each other, condemned slaves, or wild animals.

c. 275 BCE
Several **Celtic** tribes had established themselves in Britain, including the Brigantes, the Iceni, and the Corieltauvi.

Celts were originally several tribes living in central Europe from the 6th century BCE. They spread and settled all over Europe in the 3rd century BCE, from Turkey in the east to Portugal in the west. Celtic groups shared similar languages and a polytheistic religion. Early Celts left no written records.

250 BCE

272 BCE
Ashoka the Great began his rule of the Mauryan Indian Empire, which replaced the Maghada Empire of Chandragupta. At its height, it stretched from Iran through most of India. Later, Ashoka turned against war and converted to Buddhism, which he then promoted in India.

264–241 BCE
The first of the three **Punic Wars** were fought between Rome and Carthage, a Phoenician city in North Africa (now Tunis) that was the main power in the Mediterranean. It was the largest naval war of the ancient world.

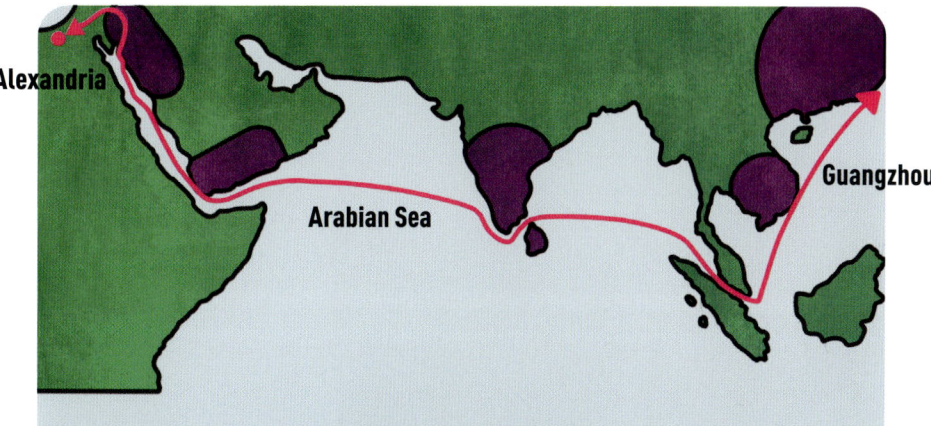

250 BCE–250 CE
Arab traders used a sea route between Alexandria in Egypt and Guangzhou in China.

THE ANCIENT WORLD

249–150 BCE

China began to emerge as one of the major powers on Earth. Becoming a single state with a huge population, it forged its own way with only limited contact with the world outside. China followed an isolationist (staying alone) policy for much of its history, limiting trade with other states. Meanwhile, Rome was growing in importance and power in Europe.

221 BCE

Shi Huangdi unified China, starting the first imperial dynasty, the **Qin**. He removed borders between states and built roads and canals, which made trade and movement easier. Worried about losing power, he strengthened the army and his own position, until by 213 BCE China was like a police state, with every aspect of life controlled. He had books of Confucian philosophy burned, and 460 Confucian scholars executed in 213 BCE.

210 BCE

Shi died and was buried with an army of **terracotta warriors** in a booby-trapped tomb. He had been obsessed with immortality, and probably died after taking a poisonous potion that was meant to help him live forever.

249 BCE

Hannibal's war elephants crossing the mountains in northern Italy

218 BCE

At the start of the **Second Punic War**, the Carthaginian general, Hannibal, crossed the Alps to attack Rome, taking an army with war elephants.

216 BCE

Hannibal's army wiped out the largest Roman army ever amassed, killing over 45,000 soldiers at Cannae—around nine times Hannibal's losses. Even so, Rome won the war.

The three Punic Wars were fought between Rome and Carthage—then the main power in the Mediterranean. Carthage managed the wars badly and lost all three. A peace treaty lasted for nearly 50 years, but Rome attacked Carthage in 146 BCE, burning it to the ground. Rome controlled the state for nearly 600 years.

210–207 BCE

Emperor Qin Er Shi initiated the building of the **Great Wall of China**.

THE ANCIENT WORLD

200 BCE–600 CE
The Nazca civilization in Peru cut huge **patterns into the surface of the desert**. These can only be seen clearly from above. Their purpose is unknown, but they were possibly walked around during ceremonial processions.

Designs in the Nazca lines include a hummingbird and a monkey

196 BCE
The **Rosetta Stone** was carved in Egypt, giving the same text in three different languages: Egyptian hieroglyphs, Demotic, and Greek. Jean-François Champollion deciphered hieroglyphs in the 1820s by studying the Stone.

150 BCE

2ND CENTURY BCE
The Indian cavalry used a **toe stirrup**, which held the big toe in a leather strap. It wasn't attached to the saddle, but was thrown over the back of the horse.

200 BCE
The Zapotec culture (500 BCE–900 CE) left some of the **earliest writing from Mesoamerica**. The writing is found on "conquest slabs," recording places that had been conquered.

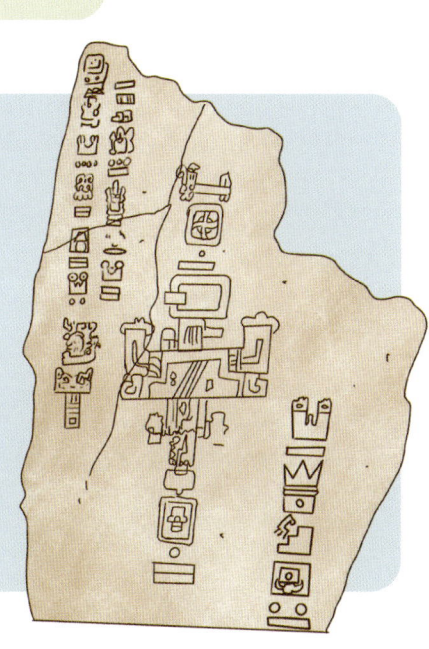

2ND CENTURY BCE
People carved the first **Buddhist art** into the cave monasteries and worship-halls of Ajanta in central India. The carvings represent stories from Buddhist texts and the previous incarnations of the Buddha.

THE ANCIENT WORLD

149–1 BCE

Rome and China continued to develop. In China, an advanced civil service ran the state efficiently, and philosophy, art, and technology flourished. From the 1st century BCE, China led the world in some areas—although its isolation meant new knowledge was not quickly shared. Rome focused on taking over new lands. In military strategy, training, technology, and making infrastructure such as roads, Rome was unrivalled.

The Silk Routes were trade routes that linked the Near East and Europe with the Far East. They extended from Antioch in Turkey across the Syrian desert and Iraq, then eastward through Iran, Turkmenistan, and Afghanistan to Mongolia and China.

125 BCE
Diplomat Zhang Qian returned to China with news of western Asia. His expedition in 138–126 BCE helped open up China to trade with the outside world along the **Silk Routes**.

The Silk Routes linked China and the Mediterranean

64 BCE
Rome annexed Syria, extending the Silk Routes westward to the Mediterranean.

149 BCE

124 BCE
An imperial university was opened to train people for the **Chinese civil service**. The civil service ran the country, following the directions of the emperor. Working for it was a desirable job. Rooted in Confucian ideas, it set the pattern of Chinese policy for 2,000 years.

73–71 BCE
The gladiator **Spartacus** led the largest slave revolt of ancient Rome. He plotted with around 70 other slaves to escape the gladiator compound. Outside, he gathered an army of 120,000 further slaves and marched against Rome. The war lasted for three years before Spartacus was defeated and the remaining slaves were slaughtered.

146 BCE
The Roman army defeated Carthage in the **Third Punic War**. They looted and burned the city, taking the inhabitants as slaves. The land stood more or less empty until the Roman Dictator Julius Caesar planned a new Carthage 100 years later.

107 BCE
The **Roman army** was restructured and turned into a professional army with well-equipped soldiers, each fully trained and carrying their own equipment.

58–50 BCE
In the Gallic Wars, **Julius Caesar** attacked and finally took over Gaul—France, Belgium, Germany, and Switzerland. He sent troops into England, subduing the tribes there and gaining tribute (payment) and slaves.

THE ANCIENT WORLD

1st CENTURY BCE
The oldest surviving **Buddhist stupa** at Sanchi, first built in the 3rd century BCE, was repaired and enlarged. A stupa is a mound-shaped structure containing sacred relics, and is used as a place for meditation.

48 BCE
Cleopatra fought against her brother (and husband) Ptolemy XIII to become sole ruler of Egypt. She won, in part thanks to an alliance with Julius Caesar.

44 BCE
Julius Caesar, newly declared "dictator forever," was **murdered** by a group of senators. They feared the Roman Republic was threatened by him taking so much power.

27 BCE
The Roman Empire was established, overturning the Republic, with **Caesar Augustus** as the first emperor. He is often considered one of the greatest leaders in history.

1 BCE

1st CENTURY BCE
The Mesoamerican Maya developed a **52-year calendar**.

A circular calendar called the "tzolkin" shows the 260-day cycle central to the Mayan calendar

c. 20 BCE
King Herod began rebuilding the **temple in Jerusalem**, making it much larger. It survived only until 70 CE when Roman invaders destroyed it.

c. 6 BCE
Jesus Christ was born in Bethlehem. In Christian tradition, he is seen as the son of God, while for Jews he was a prophet. In 525 CE, the church estimated the date of Jesus' birth as 1 CE instead, giving us the BC/AD or BCE/CE system of marking time. There is no year 0.

THE ANCIENT WORLD

RISE OF THE ROMAN EMPIRE

Rome began as a single city near the west coast of Italy, yet by the end of the 1st century CE it ruled 30 percent of the world's population—4–5 million people.

ROMAN REPUBLIC

In 509 BCE, the last king of Rome, Tarquinius, was overthrown at the end of a long process of change. The city-state was then ruled by the "patricians," the men of notable, wealthy families. This annoyed the other citizens, who objected. After 494 BCE, power was shared among more (male) citizens. Over time, a complicated structure developed of assemblies and elected officials who governed Rome and decided its laws and policies. It had become a **Republic**.

The purple zone is the largest area ruled by the Roman Empire

THE RISE OF ROME

Originally, Italy was a collection of city-states that fought over land and borders. Rome forced men into military service, and by 275 BCE the army had taken over most of Italy and developed methods of war that made it unbeatable. Rome grew to be the main power in the Mediterranean after the defeat of **Carthage** in the Punic Wars (264–146 BCE) and of **Greece** in the Macedonian Wars (214–148 BCE).

A MILITARY POWER

The **Roman army** was divided into troops trained and organized for different types of fighting, with carefully thought-out tactics and a tiered structure of leadership. There were three levels of foot soldiers (legionaries) and then cavalry (horse-riding soldiers). Soldiers were sent into battle in increasing order of expertise and weaponry, saving the best warriors for last. This meant the enemy were hit by increasingly experienced fresh troops during a battle.

From 107 BCE, the commander **Gaius Marius** made huge changes to the army. For the first time, soldiers didn't have to own property or buy their own weapons and armor, but were trained and equipped with a spear and sword by the state. It became a regular standing army, growing quickly as men flocked to join. The soldiers were grouped into four legions of 6,000 men each. Each carried his own equipment, removing the need for a baggage train. Gaius Marius recruited soldiers from conquered lands, who often had special skills suited to fighting in their own regions.

In the "tortoise" formation, groups of foot soldiers went into battle fully protected in front and above by large shields

FROM REPUBLIC TO EMPIRE

The reform of the army had some unplanned results. Soldiers relied on their generals for payment, and became more loyal to them than to the state. Power struggles between generals became common. Corruption and threats led to three men forming a "triumvirate" to take control of Rome: **Julius Caesar**, **Pompey**, and **Crassus**. But it didn't last. Crassus was killed in battle, and Pompey died when he went to war with Julius Caesar. The survivor, Caesar, was declared dictator (sole ruler). When he was murdered, the Republic collapsed and gave way to the **Roman Empire**. The first emperor, in 27 BCE, was Caesar's stepson, **Augustus**.

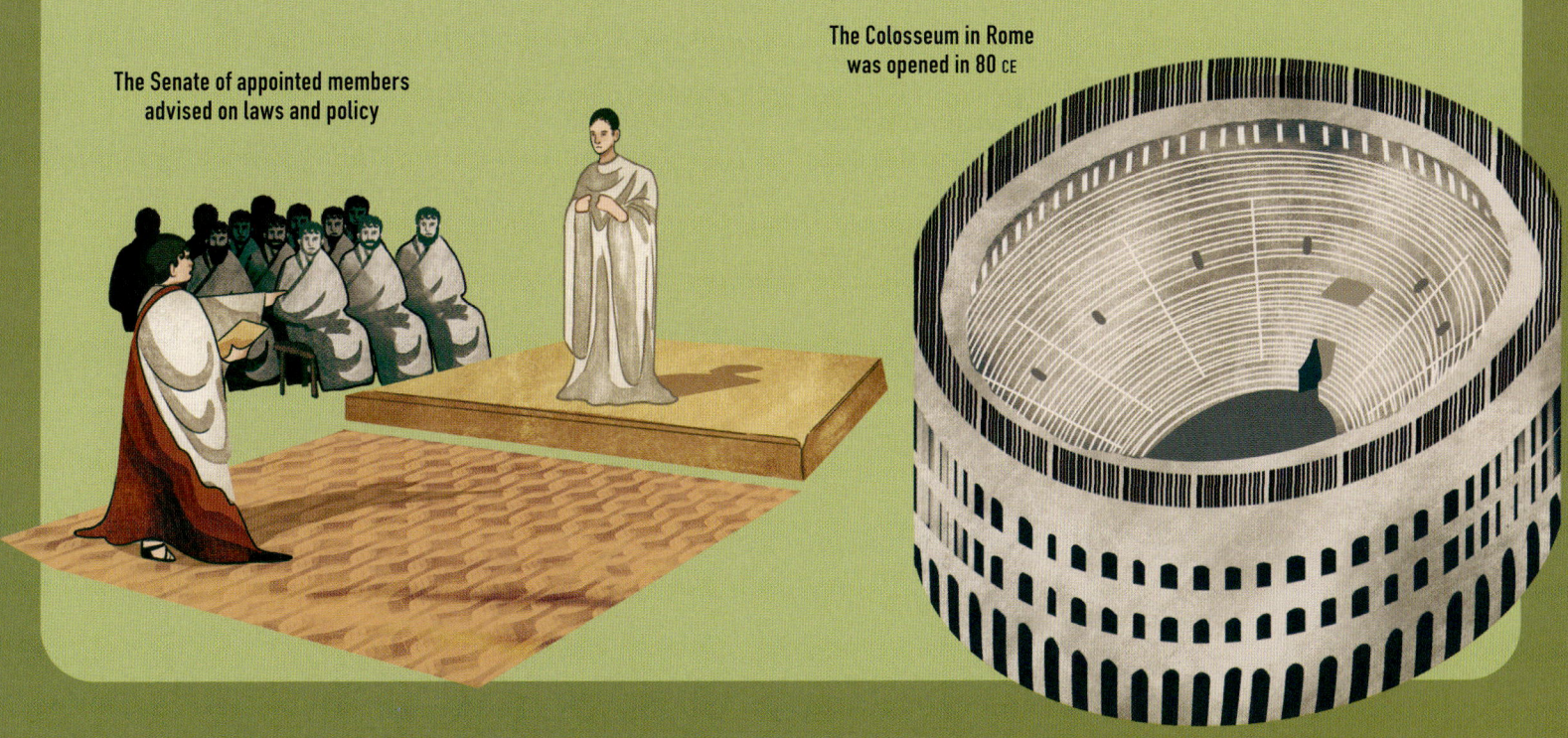

The Senate of appointed members advised on laws and policy

The Colosseum in Rome was opened in 80 CE

ROMAN EUROPE

The Roman Empire prospered for a long time, reaching its height in 117 CE as the **largest empire of the western world**. The Romans built good-quality roads throughout their conquered lands, aqueducts to carry water channels, and buildings that in some cases have lasted until today. They spread the Latin language and Roman civilization throughout their empire, from northern England to Turkey and North Africa.

THE ANCIENT WORLD

1–250 CE

Europe was still dominated by the Roman Empire, but the Romans were threatened by the Gauls and other groups in the lands they had conquered. Meanwhile, new cultures sprang up in in the Americas and sub-Saharan Africa. They left few records, but their art and engineering projects reveal their skills.

1–800
The **Moche** culture in northern Peru is famed for its art, particularly metalwork and pottery. A sophisticated network of canals and aqueducts carried the water needed for farming.

60
The Celtic queen of the Iceni tribe in Britain, **Boudicca**, led an uprising against the Romans. She destroyed their headquarters at Camulodunum (Colchester) and burned the cities of Verulamium (St Albans) and Londinium (London), killing 80,000 Roman citizens. But the Romans defeated the Iceni the following year.

79
The Roman cities of Pompeii and Herculaneum were completely destroyed by an eruption of the volcano **Mount Vesuvius**. Buried completely under volcanic ash and rock, the cities were rediscovered 1,600 years later.

1 CE

c. 30
Christ was crucified outside Jerusalem. Christ's disciple, Peter, became the leader of a small band of Christians.

43
The Roman army successfully **invaded Britain** during the rule of the emperor Claudius.

64
The city of **Rome burned down**, the fire possibly started by the emperor Nero. Nero was a corrupt and cruel emperor who allegedly murdered his own mother and two wives.

100
The kingdom of **Aksum** was founded in Africa. In the 3rd–6th centuries, it covered land in Ethiopia, Eritrea, Djibouti, Somalia, and Somaliland. Its success was built on agriculture and control of routes used to trade in gold and ivory.

100
Buddhism spread from India into China along the Silk Route.

THE ANCIENT WORLD

100
The **Hopewell** culture was established in North America, and spread through the Mississippi valley. The Hopewell made impressive ceramics, art, and technology, including irrigation ditches and intricate mounds, some shaped like animals and others in geometric shapes. The mounds can only be clearly distinguished from above.

Hopewell art

122
The Roman Emperor **Hadrian** had a wall built across the north of England to keep the Caledonians in Scotland out of Roman-occupied Britain.

Roman soldiers patrolled Hadrian's Wall

250 CE

c. 105
Good-quality **paper** was invented in China. Earlier paper made from hemp had been used since the 2nd century BCE. The new, fine paper led to an increase in writing and literacy, and established painting using a brush and ink as a dominant artform in China. Paper was also used to make hats, armor, and even windows.

Making paper

c. 150
The Greek-Egyptian astronomer **Ptolemy** described a geocentric system with Earth in the middle of the solar system. It remained the standard model for nearly 1,500 years.

166
The first recorded visit of a **Roman mission to China** took place, traveling by sea.

Compass — Rocket powered by gunpowder

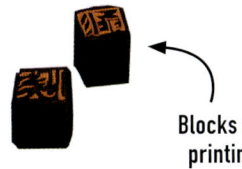

Blocks for printing

China produced four world-changing inventions, of which paper was the first. The others were the compass used for navigation (by the 11th century CE), gunpowder, and printing. The invention of printing created more demand for paper.

250–538
The state of **Yamato** expanded to cover around half the area of modern Japan. Local leaders were often persuaded to join the growing state in exchange for positions of power, although sometimes military force was used.

THE ANCIENT WORLD

251–450 CE

The might of the Roman Empire was challenged from within and outside. The Huns, perhaps originally from Kazakhstan, proved terrifying for everyone they met as they swept through Europe, pushing waves of migrants westward and causing confrontations with the Romans.

284
Diocletian become Roman emperor, and shortly afterward divided his territories into eastern and western halves. The **Eastern Roman Empire** is sometimes called the Byzantine Empire after its capital in Byzantium (now Istanbul).

EARLY 4TH CENTURY
Paired **stirrups** were used in China. They helped riders stay on a horse's back and control the animal. The use of stirrups spread westward with the nomadic tribes of Central Asia.

251 CE

312
Emperor Constantine adopted **Christianity** and began to promote it in the Western Roman Empire. Christianity had previously been outlawed.

319–467
The **Gupta Empire** covered much of India, absorbing smaller states under the leadership of Chandragupta and then his son, Samudragupta. It was a golden age for India, with achievements in literature, sculpture, architecture, astronomy, and medicine.

313
Constantine defeated the Eastern Roman Empire in battle, reuniting the empire. He moved the capital to Byzantium, which he rebuilt in 324–330 CE and renamed **Constantinople**.

Constantine added Roman features to Constantinople, including a hippodrome (arena for horse-racing)

350
The **Kingdom of Kush ended** after 1,000 years, attacked by Aksum. Its fall was hastened by climate change and rebellion.

THE ANCIENT WORLD

370
Nomadic tribes of **Huns** moved from the Steppe toward Europe, driving the **Goths** west into Germany and Hungary. The Huns and Goths formed part of the "barbarian" hordes that Romans saw as a threat to their civilization. These nomadic people left no written records, so we don't have their side of the story.

375–500
In Mexico, the city **Teotihuacan** was at its height in this period with a population of 100,000–200,000. It had many large buildings, including dramatic pyramids and temples. Little is known of the people and their beliefs. Their glyph-based script recorded only names and dates.

One of the gods worshipped in Teotihuacan was Quetzalcoatl, a feathered serpent

c. 400
Polynesian settlers arrived in **Hawaii** from the Marquesas Islands, 3,200 km (2,000 miles) away. They remained isolated from other cultures until 1778.

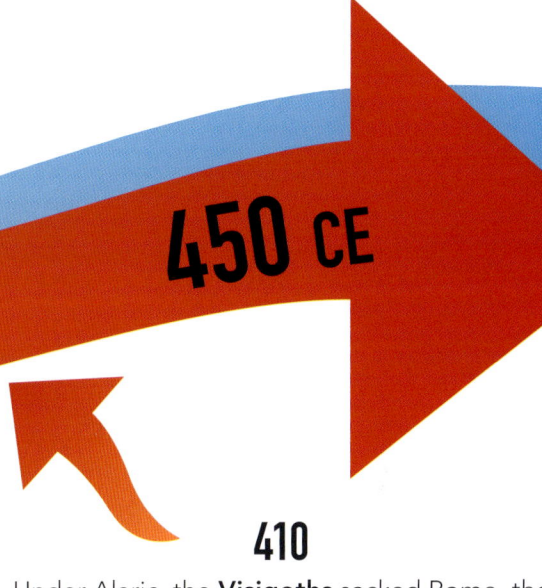

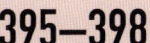 **450 CE**

376
Prompted by Roman mistreatment, the Visigoths (originally from central Europe) attacked Roman towns. They defeated the Romans at Adrianople in 378 CE, killing the emperor Valens. Historians consider this the beginning of the **fall of the Roman Empire**.

395–398
The **Huns** invaded Roman land in the east, destroying everything in their path and driving other tribes before them. Expert horsemen, the Huns were fast and brutal, and the Romans were unable to defend themselves against them.

410
Under Alaric, the **Visigoths** sacked Rome, the first intruders to enter the city in 800 years. Roman settlements throughout Europe came under attack.

Attila the Hun (ruled 434–453 CE) built an empire stretching from Central Asia to France. Accounts of the Huns come from their enemies, who recorded a fearsome reputation for savagery. After ransacking the Eastern Roman Empire, Attila attacked the Western Empire in 451 CE and the next year marched into Italy. He stopped short of Rome, though, and returned to his base in Hungary. He died in 453 CE and was buried in a secret place that has never been discovered. By 469 CE, his vast empire had fallen apart.

THE ANCIENT WORLD

451–632 CE

China and Japan flourished. Under the Tang emperors, China made great advances in science, philosophy, politics, and literature, while Japan gained a stable basis for its government. The Grand Canal in China helped to link different parts of the huge state. In the Middle East, the teachings of Muhammad saw the start of the Muslim religion, Islam.

455
The **Vandals**, a group originally from Scandinavia and perhaps Poland, attacked and looted Rome, but did not destroy the city.

476
The Western Roman Empire ended when the general, **Odoacer**, overthrew the young emperor Romulus Augustulus and made himself king.

526
The city of **Antioch** in Turkey was **destroyed** by an earthquake followed by fires that ripped through the city in the days afterward. Around a quarter of a million people died.

539
Emperor Kinmei was the first historically confirmed emperor of Japan. According to legend, there had been 29 previous emperors over the last 1,000 years, but there is no historical evidence for them. Kinmei introduced Buddhism into Japan in 552 CE after the king of Korea sent him a golden Buddha.

451 CE

6TH CENTURY CE
An early form of **chess**, called chaturanga, was first played in the Gupta Empire in India. It had only four of the modern pieces, but the game evolved over time.

536–560
A series of **volcanic eruptions** threw dust and ash into the atmosphere, blocking sunlight in the worst "volcanic winter" of the last 2,000 years. Cold, fog, and drought caused crop failure and famine around the world.

6TH CENTURY CE
The number of **monasteries** in Europe increased. Monks copied the Bible by hand.

604
Prince Shōtoku of Japan is said to have written the Seventeen-Article Constitution, which sets out the qualities and values that help people run a country smoothly. Shōtoku promoted Chinese culture and Buddhism, trying to bring Japan closer to China.

THE ANCIENT WORLD

c. 610

Work began on extensions and improvements to the **Grand Canal in China**. It was the most ambitious civil engineering project in the world until the Industrial Revolution.

No body has been found in the Sutton Hoo burial

c. 610–635

An Anglo-Saxon longship was buried at **Sutton Hoo** in England, loaded with treasure. Beautiful objects made locally and brought from as far away as Turkey and India show the skill of Anglo-Saxon craft workers, and the extent of foreign trade at the time.

c. 613

The prophet Muhammad began preaching the message of Allah in Mecca, leading to the founding of **Islam**.

632 CE

618

The **Tang dynasty** began in China. It lasted until 907 CE and was one of the greatest, bringing reform of the political system and advances in art, science, and technology. The first Tang emperor, Goazu, created the legal code that still underlies Chinese law. He protected the peasants from too much tax and redistributed land more fairly.

Goazu, the first Tang emperor, ruled 618–626 CE

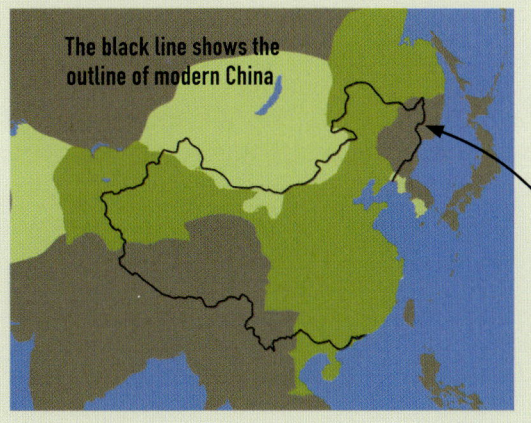

The black line shows the outline of modern China

Areas controlled by the Tang dynasty are shown in dark green. Other empires are shown in light green.

622

Muhammad moved from Mecca to Medina, where he had been asked to come and solve old disputes between Arabs and Jews. Most of Muhammad's Muslim followers went with him in an event known in Islam as the **Hegira** (migration). The Muslim calendar starts with the year AH1, corresponding to 622 CE.

632

Muhammad died in Medina, probably of a fever.

CHAPTER 3

THE MIDDLE AGES

The period between the death of Muhammad and 1400 saw the "Old World" of Europe, Asia, and Africa becoming much more connected, but there were still no links between the Old World and the Americas or Australasia. This period, commonly called the Middle Ages, saw huge changes in much of the world. Struggles between Islam and Christianity played out in the Middle East. In the Far East, China, Japan, and Korea forged identities that have shaped them as modern nations. It was a time of empire-building on a grand scale, and often bitter warfare.

The Mongol Empire stretched from China to the middle of Europe at its height, and much of West Africa fell under the control of the Mali Empire. Europe became Christian, and launched a terrible assault on the Muslim Arabs—a century of "Crusades" to claim the holy area of Jerusalem and Israel as their own. But the most turmoil came at the end of the period, with the Black Death, a deadly pandemic that swept through Europe and parts of Asia, killing millions.

— THE MIDDLE AGES —

633–749 CE

In the years after the death of Muhammad, the Muslim Arabs of the Rashidun Caliphate continued the expansion that Muhammad had begun. They became the leading power in West Asia. At the same time, the Vikings started raiding European coastal areas from the north.

633–656

From modern-day Saudi Arabia, **Muslim Arabs** attacked the Sassanian Empire in Iraq and the Byzantine Empire in Syria. They captured Syria, Jordan, and Palestine in 636, Egypt in 640–642, and the Mediterranean islands of Cyprus and Rhodes. Expansion stopped in 656 CE with civil war in the empire.

661–750

Under the **Umayyad Caliphate**, Muslim Arabs extended their empire into North Africa and beyond: the Iberian Peninsula (in 711–714), and parts of Italy, Greece, eastern Europe, and Pakistan. The Umayyads brutally crushed all uprisings and civil wars.

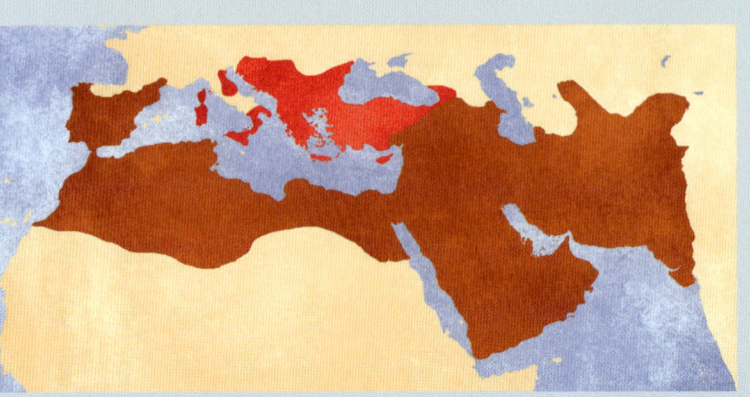

- Umayyad Empire
- Territory seized from the Byzantine Empire

The full extent of the Umayyad Empire in 732 CE

633 CE

637

Jerusalem surrendered to the Muslims, and Jews were allowed to return to the city, 500 years after being sent away by the Romans.

c. 650

A **slave trade** operated between sub-Saharan Africa and the Arab world. Around 6 million people were captured or bought from local rulers and sent to slave markets in Egypt, Morocco, Algiers, and Constantinople (modern-day Istanbul).

LATE 7TH CENTURY CE

Vikings from Scandinavia developed **longships**, adding sails to the boats with oars. This made the ships quick enough for the Vikings' deadly raids on coastland.

690–705

Wu Zetian reigned as the only female emperor of China. She started in a lowly position in court, looking after laundry, but married an emperor and ruled after his death. She reformed the administration, farming, education, the military, and even the language, keen to make her rule a new start for China.

THE MIDDLE AGES

c. 691
The **Dome of the Rock** was completed on the Temple Mount, Jerusalem. It was built over the "foundation stone" that was important to both Islam and Judaism.

The present tiles and gold on the Dome of the Rock are more recent

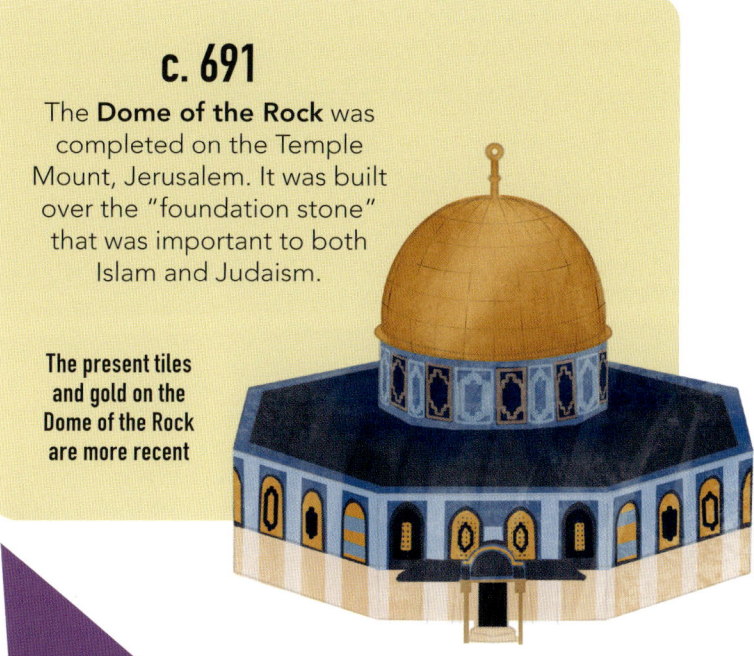

711–714
The North African Berber leader, Tāriq ibn Ziyād, captured Spain and Portugal from the Visigoths for the Umayyad Caliphate. The territory, called **al-Andalus**, remained under Muslim Arab rule until the 11th century.

6th–7th CENTURIES
The Indo-Arabic **numerals**, which include the digits 1–9, were first used in India.

735–737
Several waves of **smallpox** spread through Japan, killing 25–35 percent of the population.

749 CE

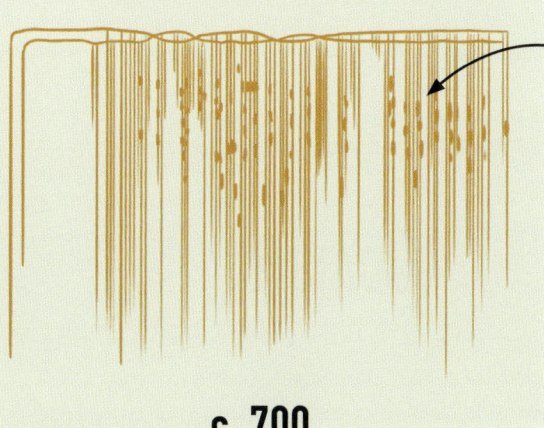

The "language" of the early quipu hasn't been deciphered

c. 700
The Wari culture used the **quipu**, a system of knotted strings to represent numbers and probably words. The **Wari Empire**, the first in South America, lasted from 600–1000. The Wari left a road network and style of earthquake-proof buildings that influenced the later Incas.

718
Byzantine emperor Leo III used **Greek fire** to put an end to the siege of Constantinople by Umayyad forces. We don't know exactly what was in Greek fire, but it may have included petroleum and sulfur.

732
Charles Martel halted the Muslim invasion of France at the **Battle of Tours**.

c. 725
In France, the ruler Charles Martel gave lands to the nobles and laid the foundations of **feudal law**.

Tōdai-ji was the largest wooden temple in the world

745–752
Tōdai-ji ("Great Eastern Temple") was built as an offering after the smallpox epidemic. Its cost nearly bankrupted Japan.

THE MIDDLE AGES

LASTING RELIGIONS

Early religions were often polytheistic (meaning they have many gods), and some focused on spirits in streams, trees, and other natural features. Of the religions that have survived, most are monotheistic (they have one god), and many became established in 350 BCE to 650 CE.

ZOROASTRIANISM

Zoroastrianism began between 1500 BCE and 1000 BCE in Iran, founded by the Persian prophet **Zoroaster** who was enlightened by a vision. Its single god, **Ahura Mazda**, is worshipped through good thoughts, good words, and good deeds. Zoroastrianism grew from a polytheistic religion in which Ahura Mazda was the chief god. Zoroaster's teachings were passed down by word of mouth until the 6th century BCE, when they were written down. Zoroastrianism had a heaven and hell, a judgment day at the end of time, and other aspects adopted by later religions, including Christianity and Islam.

The Zoroastrian god Ahura Mazda

Yahweh spoke to Moses from a burning bush, commanding him to lead the Israelites out of Egypt

JUDAISM

Early Judaism (the religion of the Jews) separated from older Israelite religions sometime in the 6th century BCE, leaving **Yahweh** as the only god by the 3rd century BCE. The Hebrew Bible tells the history of the Israelites, starting with the creation of the world, and sets down the laws by which Jews must live. The most important prophets in Judaism are **Abraham** and **Moses**. Yahweh gave Moses the most important laws, the Ten Commandments, written on stone tablets.

THE MIDDLE AGES

CHRISTIANITY

Christianity started after the death of **Jesus Christ** around 30 CE. The Christian **Bible** consists of the Old and New Testaments, the second of which records the life of Jesus Christ. The Old Testament is shared with Judaism. Christians consider Christ to be the **Messiah**, sent to free humankind and cleanse them of sin, fulfilling a prophesy in the Old Testament. Jews consider Christ to be another prophet, and believe that the Messiah has not yet come.

A Byzantine mosaic of Christ

ISLAM

Islam shares Old Testament stories with Judaism and Christianity, but sees **Muhammad** as the last prophet sent by God (**Allah**). **Muslims** (followers of Islam) believe that Allah dictated the holy **Quran** to Muhammad in the 7th century CE. Other important prophets were Abraham, Moses, and Jesus. Muslims are taught to pray daily, give to charity, fast during the month of Ramadan, and go on a pilgrimage to Mecca at least once.

A pilgrimage to the Kaaba, or House of God, in Mecca, is called "hajj." The Kaaba is a cube-shaped building in the middle of the Masjid al-Haram mosque.

BUDDHISM

Buddhism began in India in the 5th century BCE with the teachings of the **Buddha**, a prince who left his life of luxury and went out into the world to seek truth. Prompted by seeing the sufferings of ordinary people, the prince meditated and sought nlightenment, which came to him as he sat under a tree. He spent the rest of his life teaching people to live a virtuous life. Buddhists try to live according to the teachings of Buddha.

HINDUISM

Hinduism is a diverse and varied religion that began around 2000 BCE in the Indus Valley. The main god is **Brahman**, who Hindus believe is present everywhere and takes many forms. His most important forms are as creator (**Brahma**), preserver of the world (**Vishnu**), and destroyer (**Shiva**). Hindus believe in a cycle of life, death, and rebirth, and that the world is periodically destroyed and renewed. Hinduism has several sacred texts, including stories of the gods and hymns of praise.

THE MIDDLE AGES

750–849 CE

The 8th and 9th centuries saw the growing power of the Islamic Arab caliphate and the rise of the Franks and the Vikings in Europe. They filled the gap left by the Romans, battling to take over areas of Europe that were ruled by small, warring groups.

768
When Pepin III died, the Frankish Empire was divided between his sons, Carloman and Charlemagne. In 771, Carloman died and **Charlemagne** took over the entire empire.

750
Abbasid rebels massacred the Umayyads in Damascus, finally overthrowing them and starting a new caliphate. They made their capital in **Baghdad**. The first two caliphs, as-Saffah and al-Mansur, committed many atrocities.

Over 46 years, Charlemagne extended the Frankish Empire from northern Spain to parts of Germany, Italy, and Hungary, his mission was to conquer and to spread Christianity. He declared himself leader of the Church and was crowned Emperor of the Holy Roman Empire by the Pope in 800. He encouraged the spread of literacy (reading) and continued improvements in agriculture and technology started under Pepin. These included rotating crops between fields on a three-year cycle, which increased yield by around a third. Charlemagne is sometimes called the "father" of modern Europe.

Charlemagne being crowned by Pope Leo III

750 CE

c. 750–1000
Over the course of a few centuries, the Maya civilization experienced a cultural shift known as the "Maya Collapse." Many major Maya cities were abandoned and society fell apart. Historians argue over why this happened, but it was likely a combination of overpopulation, droughts, warfare, and political instability.

756
The **Emirate of Córdoba** (in Spain) was started by Abd al-Rahman I, who escaped the Abbasid slaughter in the Muslim Empire. The Emirate eventually covered most of Spain. It was central to European learning and scholarship in the Middle Ages.

c. 770
Arab scholars in a great library and school in Baghdad, the **House of Wisdom**, collected and translated Ancient Greek, Syrian, Persian, and Indian texts into Arabic. These works formed the basis of medieval Arab scholarship.

751
In France, Pepin III was crowned king of the Franks, starting the great **Carolingian dynasty**. He expanded Frankish territory.

Scholars in the House of Wisdom

THE MIDDLE AGES

c. 795
Viking raids on Scotland began, and continued for hundreds of years. The Vikings sailed from Norway, raiding seaports around Europe and settling in areas of France, Italy, Britain, and Iceland. Later, the Vikings reached North America.

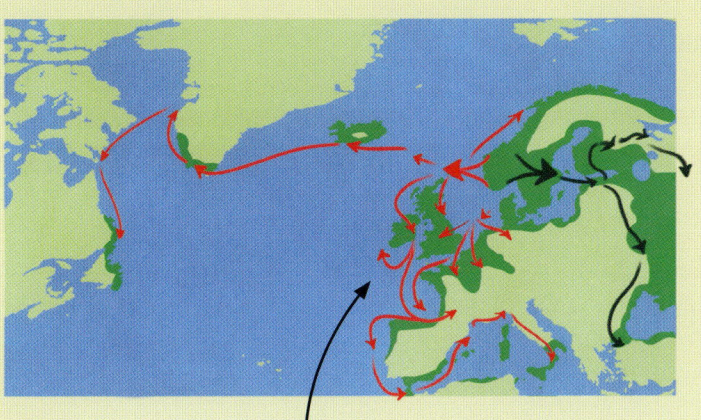

Routes taken by Vikings from Norway and Denmark (red arrows) and Sweden (blue arrows)

A pottery container filled with gunpowder was an early hand grenade

9TH CENTURY CE
In China, alchemists discovered how to make **gunpowder**. It had a massive impact on warfare, bringing terrifying new, powerful weapons. The Chinese tried to keep the recipe secret, but the Arabs discovered it around 1240–1280.

849 CE

794–1185
The **Fujiwara** clan dominated Japan. The women married emperors and princes, then appointed Fujiwara men as regents, ruling while emperors were still young. In this way, the clan built strong family ties with the emperors and effectively ruled Japan.

c. 800–MID-16TH CENTURY
The **Muisca** civilization in Columbia were accomplished goldworkers. Their work probably prompted the myth of El Dorado, a fabled city of gold, which led the conquistadors (Spanish invaders) to ravage South America in the 1500s.

A Muisca golden raft made around 800 CE

9TH–11TH CENTURIES CE
The **Ghana Empire** was at its height. It thrived because it had a well-trained army and access to metals for making weapons and trading. Ghana dominated trade in West Africa from the 7th century, particularly in gold, iron, ivory, hides, feathers, and enslaved people.

802
The **Khmer Empire** was established in Cambodia. It lasted until 1431, and at its peak, covered Cambodia, Thailand, Laos, and southern Vietnam.

THE MIDDLE AGES

850–999 CE

In Europe, new power blocs took shape, with the Magyars in Hungary, and the Vikings settling as Normans in France. Life was perilous for poorer people in less-organized states. Many people were captured in eastern Europe and sold into slavery, and in France and England a feudal system relied on serfs whose position was little different from slavery.

Feudal land was divided into small strips rather than large fields

856
The fifth-deadliest **earthquake** ever recorded killed 200,000 people in Damghan, Iran.

895/6
Magyars crossed the Carpathian Mountains and settled in sparsely populated Moravian territory, from where they launched raids around Europe. They became the core of the Hungarian people. The **Kingdom of Hungary** was created in 1000.

907
The great **Tang dynasty** in China **came to an end** after 80 years of uprisings, rebellions, assassinations, and chaos.

850 CE

Smallpox was highly infectious

868
The **Diamond Sutra** was made—the world's oldest printed book. It's a sequence of Buddhist texts in Chinese, printed on paper made into a scroll.

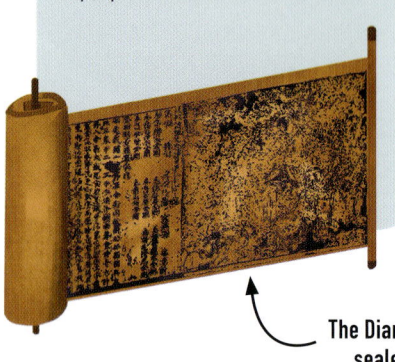

The Diamond Sutra was found sealed in a cave in 1900

10TH CENTURY CE
The Japanese medical text *Ishinpō* advised setting up **isolation hospitals** for patients with smallpox, suggesting that people knew it was contagious—even though they also thought it was caused by angry gods.

911
After years of raids on French territory, the Viking chieftain Rollo was recognized as the rightful ruler of part of Normandy. The **Norman Vikings** gained more territory, became Christian, and by 990 Normandy was French-speaking.

THE MIDDLE AGES

Slavery was common throughout Europe and North Africa. Christian countries had laws forbidding the sale of Christians into slavery in Muslim lands, which meant trade to Arab countries was largely from pagan Scandinavia and eastern Europe. Many Slavs were sold, often traded through Italy to Arab countries, giving us the word "slave."

People captured from northern and eastern Europe were sold into slavery

c. 950–c. 1250

The so-called **Medieval Warm Period** produced slightly raised temperatures in Europe. A warmer climate helped Vikings sail to and settle in Greenland and North America.

960

The start of the **Song dynasty** saw China reunited. A period of chaos followed the fall of the Tang dynasty, with the country being split into 10 kingdoms. Eventually, the warlord Zhao Kuangyin conquered enough kingdoms to declare himself emperor.

999 CE

Foot-binding aimed to make the feet just 10 cm (4 in) long

937–975

The process of **foot-binding** began in China, and continued until the early 20th century. It involved permanently mutilating women's feet by bending the toes beneath and binding them into a short, arched, triangular shape from the age of around five.

The feudal system became common in Europe. It was a way of managing local land, work, and wealth. Feudalism relied on a pledge of fealty (a promise of faithful service) between an overlord and a vassal. In exchange for protection and a strip of land to live and work on, the vassal gave the lord money or part of his harvest, and served as a soldier when necessary. The system could have several levels, with the king granting land to nobles, who granted it to lesser lords, and so on. At the bottom layer were serfs, who went with the land as though they were a possession.

982

Eric the Red sailed to Greenland when he was exiled from Iceland for murder. There, he encountered the Dorset people, the first recorded encounter with **Indigenous people of the Arctic**.

THE MIDDLE AGES

1000–1099

Hostility between Muslims and Christians grew. Christian Spain reclaimed some of the land conquered by Muslims. But the main Christian–Muslim conflict was in the Holy Land (Israel). Christian Crusaders attacked Jerusalem, seizing it from the Muslim inhabitants and claiming it as a Christian city. The conflict continued for nearly 200 years.

1030
The Tamil **Chola Empire** was at its height, ruling Sri Lanka and southern India, and with influence throughout Southeast Asia. The Chola was one of the longest-lasting dynasties in the world, believed to date back to at least the 3rd century BCE, and ruling until the 13th century.

c. 1000
Leif Erikson sailed from Greenland to North America, and probably started a colony at **Vinland** (Newfoundland).

c. 1000
The first official **paper money** was introduced widely in China, replacing independent merchants' notes.

The earliest paper money, the Chinese Jiaozi note

c. 1050–1450
The kingdom of **Ife** thrived in Niger. The Ife people smelted iron, and their culture is famous for astonishing life-size metal sculptures of human heads.

1000

1000
The **Thule** migrated eastward from Arctic Canada, reaching Greenland around 1200–1300, where they replaced the Dorset culture. The Thule—ancestors of the Inuit—dominated the far north by 1500.

BY 1021
The world's first **novel** was written in Japan. *The Tale of Genji*, by Murasaki Shikibu, tells the story of the life of the son of an emperor cast out of the imperial family.

1050–1250
Spanish Christian forces took back much territory from Arab rule. The **Reconquista** (reconquest of Spain) lasted from the 11th century until 1492.

1054
The **supernova** that caused the **Crab Nebula** was observed around the world.

The remains of the supernova of 1054 (top) today form the Crab Nebula (bottom)

THE MIDDLE AGES

1055
Tughril of the Seljuk Empire in Iraq conquered Persia, seizing Baghdad and establishing the **Seljuk dynasty**. He reduced the power of the Abbasid caliphs and used the Persian army to attack other empires in the region, trying to unite the entire Islamic world.

1095–1099
The **First Crusade** began when the Byzantine emperor lost land to the Seljuks and asked for the help of western European powers. Pope Urban II launched the First Crusade to recapture Jerusalem.

The Crusades were a series of Christian attempts to recapture the holy city of Jerusalem from Muslim occupation in 1095–1291. Christian states in Europe united in a vicious attack on the Arab states. These wars left a legacy of intolerance and distrust that continues today.

The Crusades were a shameful period of invasions, barbarity, and slaughter

1071
Seljuk troops seized **Jerusalem**.

1087
Tripiṭaka Koreana, a Korean collection of Buddhist sacred texts, were carved onto 81,340 woodblocks containing over 52 million characters. The original was destroyed in Mongol invasions in 1232, but it was recarved in 1236–1252.

1099

Halley's Comet, seen in 1066, was depicted in the Bayeux tapestry

1066
The Norman king **William** successfully invaded England—the last overseas conquest of Britain. He commissioned a large **tapestry**, started in 1080, to record the history of the conquest. The tapestry was made in Bayeux, Normandy.

1099
The **Siege of Jerusalem ended** with Christian Crusaders capturing the city and massacring most of the Jews and Muslims living there, then converting the Dome of the Rock to a Christian church.

THE MIDDLE AGES

MONGOL EMPIRE

The Mongols were tribes from the Central Asian Steppe, perhaps originating in Kazakhstan. Originally nomads, they lived on horseback and were used to the harshest weather and living conditions. This gave them a great advantage when they set out to conquer lands from China to Europe. Over the 13th century, the Mongols built the largest empire the world had ever seen.

FIRST STEPPES

Temujin (c. 1162–1227) rose from a harsh childhood to become military leader of the Kerait tribe. He drew in or conquered other tribes until a meeting of tribal leaders recognized him as **Genghis Khan**, "universal leader," in 1206. Combining the forces of all the tribes, he had a formidable army of horsemen. He adopted the script of the Uighur Turks to make a written form of Mongolian, which previously had no writing. Then he set about building an empire. His son and successor, Ogedei Khan, continued the expansion of the Mongol Empire eastward, and conquered the Kingdom of Goryeo (Korea) in 1231.

HEADING WEST

From 1218, Genghis Khan also sent his warriors westward, first sweeping through Persia, then northern Afghanistan (1221), then Russia near the Caspian Sea (1223). By the time Genghis Khan died of illness in 1227, he was known by the Muslims in conquered regions as **the accursed one**. His army was brutal and pitiless. Wherever they went, they destroyed cities and slaughtered the inhabitants, burning the buildings and wrecking irrigation systems to make farming impossible. The reputation of the Mongols for brutality meant that cities would often surrender without a fight, afraid of what would befall them otherwise.

THE MIDDLE AGES

A MIGHTY EMPIRE

Genghis Khan had wanted his four sons to rule after him, but one had already died. Of the remaining three, **Ogedei** became the great Khan and supreme ruler. He continued to expand the empire, but also strengthened the land he had. He introduced a proper system of taxes, appointed regional governors, and built a capital at Karakorum. In the east, he defeated the Jin dynasty in China and raided Korea repeatedly. In the west, the Mongols reached eastern Europe, sacking and looting Kyiv in Ukraine (1240), Kraków in Poland (1241), and Buda and Pest in Hungary (1241). Only Ogedei's death stopped them going farther west.

The Mongols were expert archers

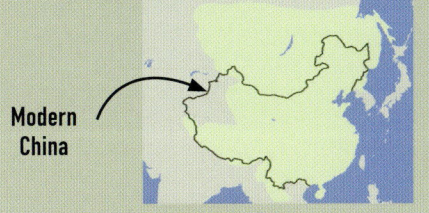

Modern China

Extent ruled by the Yuan dynasty

ANOTHER GREAT KHAN

When Genghis Khan's grandson, **Kublai**, came to power in 1260, expansion continued. Although the empire was technically still split into four, Kublai had the larger part. His heart was set on greater things, though. He attacked China, this time using siege warfare, and defeated one city after another, including the capital in 1276. With the fall of the Song dynasty, Kublai was declared emperor of China, starting the **Yuan dynasty** of occupation. Attacks on Japan were not as successful. The Japanese survived two assaults, in 1274 and 1281, when Japanese resistance and terrible storms destroyed Mongolian ships. Attacks on Vietnam, Java, and Burma were only partly successful.

DEATH OF AN EMPIRE

The four regions of the original empire slowly decayed. In eastern Europe and Russia, the **Golden Horde** (originally the northwest part of the Mongol empire) lasted longest, until 1502, but internal and border disputes ate away at all the khanates. In China, civil wars, famine, rebellion, and economic problems eventually led to the fall of the Yuan dynasty, to be replaced by the **Ming dynasty** in 1368.

THE MIDDLE AGES

1100–1299

While the Crusades continued, further bloodshed at the hands of invading Mongols marked the 13th century. First under Genghis Khan and then under his grandson Kublai Khan, fierce warriors from the Asian Steppe swept through Asia and eastern Europe, laying waste to everything that stood in their way.

1189–1192

The **Third Crusade** aimed to retake Jerusalem, but failed. Crusaders captured the city of Acre in Israel in 1191. A slaughter of prisoners on both sides followed.

1202–1204

The **Fourth Crusade** ended with the destruction and looting of Constantinople by the Crusaders. Treasure and artworks were taken by the Venetian Republic, citizens were slaughtered, and the Byzantine Empire was split up.

c. 1122–1150

The Khmer emperor Suryavarman II built the temple complex at **Angkor Wat** in Cambodia, dedicated to the Hindu god Vishnu. It is one of the largest temples in the world.

1206

Temujin took the title **Genghis Khan**, meaning "universal ruler," after uniting the Mongol tribes. He would go on to conquer a vast empire, ruthlessly killing millions.

1100

1187

Saladin, the sultan of Egypt and Syria, recaptured the city of Jerusalem from Crusaders.

1192

Minamoto no Yoritomo established the first **shogunate** (rule by military governors) to rule Japan, after defeating the rival Taira clan. The shoguns held all the military power in Japan. Controlling the army made them all-powerful until 1868. They operated a system similar to European feudalism.

Minamoto no Yoritomo

The samurai were a class of warriors that rose to power in 10th-century Japan. They were originally members of private armies gathered to protect the lands of lords who were away at the imperial court. From the Kamakura period (1192–1333), samurai became part of the military government system that evolved under the shoguns. They were accomplished soldiers, trained from a young age to fight on horseback, and use a sword and bow.

THE MIDDLE AGES

1215
King John of England was forced by the barons to sign the **Magna Carta**, which limited his power as king. It meant the king had to work within a set of laws and customs. He could not raise new taxes without consultation, and all free men accused of a crime were entitled to a fair trial.

1257
The **Samalas volcano** in Indonesia erupted, causing volcanic winter and famine around the world, and possibly triggering the "Little Ice Age" (see page 77).

1258
The Mongols **sacked Baghdad**, killing 200,000 inhabitants.

1279
The Mongols took control of all of China and established the **Yuan dynasty**, with a new capital just north of modern Beijing.

1299

1227
Batu Khan established the "Golden Horde," the vast **Mongol Empire** that stretched across much of Russia and Central Asia into eastern Europe.

1240
Sundiata Keita of the Malinke tribe founded the **Mali Empire** in West Africa. Disabled from birth, Sundiata wore iron leg braces as a child, and struggled to walk unaided. With other chiefs, Sundiata went to war with the failing Ghana Empire. He seized the capital of Ghana in 1240, beginning his empire, and continued to add new lands to it.

1250–1650
The people of Rapa Nui (Easter Island) built **giant stone statues** called moai facing toward land, with their backs to the sea. Their purpose is not known.

1250–1300
Polynesian navigators reached **New Zealand**.

1274 AND 1281
The **Kamikaze** (divine wind) destroyed two separate fleets sent by the Mongol leader Kublai Khan to invade Japan. These were the two most disastrous attempted naval landings in history.

Storms devastated the invading Mongolian fleet

THE MIDDLE AGES

1300–1399

As the Medieval Warm Period in Europe had ended and the climate grew cooler, crops grew less well, causing famines in the first half of the century. Things got worse. The middle of the century was dominated by the Black Death, a pandemic that raged through Europe and Asia.

1315–1317
Following heavy rain in the spring of 1315 and the resulting crop failure, **famine** killed millions across Europe. Some places lost up to a quarter of their population. Normal food supply did not return until 1325.

14TH CENTURY
Portolans, or coastline maps, were first developed in the late 13th century and became popular in the 14th century. They were the earliest accurate maps, used for navigating at sea.

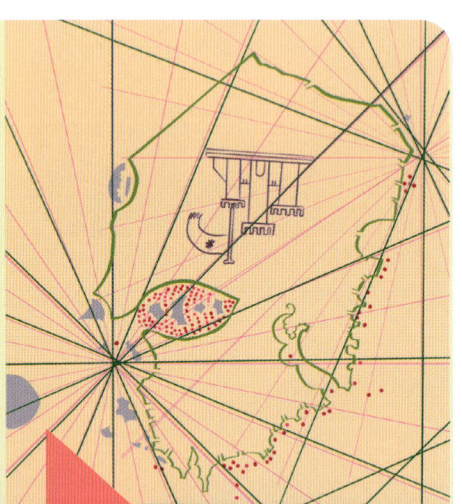

Portolan maps showed few or no details of land beyond the coast.

1325
Aztecs founded the city of **Tenochtitlan** (now the site of Mexico City). At its height, it had 200,000 inhabitants and was the largest city in Mesoamerica.

1300

The Mali Empire thrived under the rule of Mansu Musa I, 1312–1337. The ruler was known for his wealth and generosity. The city of Timbuktu became a great trading hub and was important in the spread of Islam, as African leaders and traders met Muslim Arabs. Musa doubled the size of the empire over a large area of West Africa. Only the Mongol Empire was larger at the time. When Musa stopped in Cairo en route to Mecca, his spending was so great that it is said to have caused inflation (when the prices of things go up, which means that you have to spend more money to buy the same things) and crashed the gold market. He was possibly the richest person ever to live.

1345–1347
The port of Caffa (now Feodosija, Ukraine) was besieged by Mongols. When plague broke out among the Mongol forces in 1346, they catapulted their dead over the wall, infecting the citizens of Caffa— an early act of **biological warfare**.

THE MIDDLE AGES

The Aztec Empire in Mexico lasted from 1325 to 1521, when it was destroyed by Spanish invaders. Noted for its art and architecture, including stepped pyramids, it was hugely successful, trading across Mesoamerica and controlling 11 million people. Books called codices have survived in the Aztec language, and Aztec culture was also described by the Spanish, so we know more about this civilization than many others in the early Americas.

1370
The Turkish–Mongolian leader Timur (also known as Tamerlane) founded the **Timurid Empire**, trying to recreate the Mongol Empire of Genghis Khan. With a capital in Samarkand, Uzbekistan, it extended across western central Asia, but broke up after Timur's death in 1405.

1392
Yi Seong-gye founded the **Great Joseon** (or Choson), the last dynastic kingdom in Korea, which lasted until 1910. Most of modern Korea's etiquette, language, administration, religious leanings, and customs were established during the Joseon.

c. 1346–1352
Bubonic plague (the **Black Death**) spread through Asia and Europe, killing up to half the population.

1377
The oldest surviving **book printed with movable bronze type** was made in Korea. Choe Yun-ui and his team invented the press more than 150 years before it was invented separately in Europe. It had less impact than the European press because Korean has far more characters, so printing was difficult and expensive.

1399

1368
The **Ming dynasty** replaced the Mongol Yuan dynasty in China, and lasted until 1644. The dynasty ruled over a period of population growth, wealth, and thriving art and literature.

The best-known sections of the Great Wall of China were built during the Ming dynasty

1397
The shogun Yoshimitsu built the **Golden Pavilion** in Kyoto, Japan, originally to be his retirement home. It was later converted to a Zen Buddhist temple.

THE MIDDLE AGES

BLACK DEATH

The Black Death was a pandemic of bubonic plague and its variants that spread through Asia, North Africa, and Europe in the middle of the 14th century. Around two thirds of people who caught the disease died—up to half the population in affected areas, or at least 50 million people worldwide. The effects on individuals and societies were devastating, and the population of Europe took 200 years to grow back to pre-plague levels. Outbreaks of plague continued for hundreds of years.

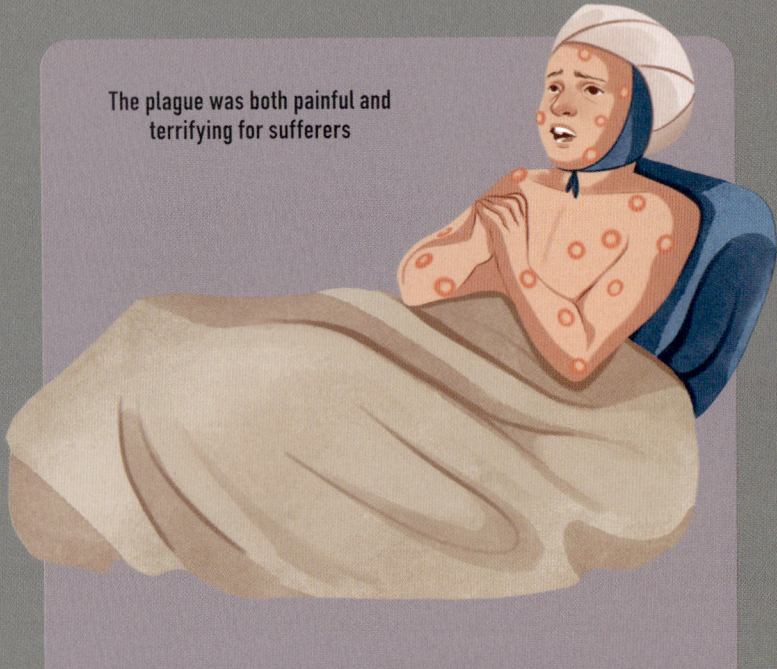

The plague was both painful and terrifying for sufferers

RATS, FLEAS, AND BOILS

Bubonic plague is a disease caused by **bacteria**. It's often spread by fleas that usually live on rats and other rodents. If a flea carrying plague bacteria bites someone, the person can catch plague. The disease can also spread directly between people, producing slightly different forms of the illness. Sufferers during the Black Death had fever and joint pain, followed by a rash, and then extremely painful boils that sometimes turned hard and black, giving the pandemic its name.

PLAGUE FROM THE EAST

The plague probably began in Central Asia, Mongolia, China, or India, and was carried east and west by Mongol warriors and traders. It entered Europe in 1347 through the Mediterranean sea ports and Crimea. It spread west and north over the next five years, leaving a **trail of devastation**. The effects were uneven, with some places barely affected, but some towns and villages entirely destroyed.

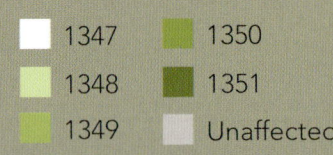

	1347		1350
1348		1351
1349		Unaffected

Plague spread from the east in 1346, taking hold over most of Europe in 1348–1350

THE MIDDLE AGES

The "Dance of Death" was a common scene in art

TERRIFYING MYSTERY

At the time, people didn't know about bacteria or understand **how diseases spread**. Many feared it was spread by "bad air," and others thought that the plague was a punishment sent by God. Some people prayed for relief, promised to build churches, or whipped themselves as a form of self-punishment to atone for past sins. The art and literature of the time shows people being aware that life was fragile and death ever-present.

People were so afraid of plague that they would flee their towns and villages to avoid it, but many carried it with them to the places they ran away to. By moving around, they **spread the plague** farther and faster. There were no effective treatments for plague at the time, though now it can be treated with antibiotics.

SOCIAL CHAOS

The effects of the pandemic were devastating. With so many dying, there were **not enough people** to dig graves for all the dead, who were piled into large pits. There were too few people to work the farms, so crops rotted or were never planted, and farm animals died or wandered away. In the years after the plague, the surviving workers could demand more money and better conditions. The feudal system relying on serfs who were tied to working the land of their overlords collapsed in many places. Serfs were replaced by peasants who could move between employers. Rebellions, food shortages, and civil unrest continued for decades after the worst of the plague was over.

Some people were buried in coffins in a ceremonial way, but many were piled into mass graves

CHAPTER 4

CONNECTING THE WORLD

The middle of the 15th century saw the start of the "Age of Discovery," when European adventurers set off across the oceans and found lands they previously knew nothing about. Using overland routes for trade between Europe and Asia was difficult, so sailors went in search of sea routes to India, China, and beyond. On the way, they found the Americas. Later explorers came across Australia.

The Europeans didn't recognize the rights of the people already living in these lands. They saw these places as new and undiscovered areas they could plunder and colonize. Invaders stole the land, killed and enslaved the inhabitants, plundered civilizations, and destroyed their cultures. At the same time, they carried animals, plants, and diseases between the "Old World" of Europe, Africa, and Asia and the "New World" of North and South America and the Caribbean islands. The invaders' unfamiliar diseases, including flu, measles, and smallpox, killed millions of people who had no resistance to them.

CONNECTING THE WORLD

1400–1484

In Europe, Asia, and South America, empires grew and shrank. The development of large ships capable of sailing across, as well as around, oceans opened up more sea routes, which were used for trade and exploration.

Ming China's isolationist policy cut it off from the outside world. There was opposition to Zheng's later journeys, and even to mentioning his trips. By the end of the century, people were banned from making ocean-going ships or leaving the country. The Ming wanted to concentrate on Chinese developments, believing nothing of value could come from outside. Instead of flourishing, Chinese culture began to stagnate.

1405–1433

The Chinese explorer and admiral **Zheng He** sailed west from China, visiting India, the Middle East, and East Africa, hoping to build trade networks. The Ming dynasty was generally isolationist, refusing contact with the world outside China. Zheng brought back knowledge, ideas, and luxury goods unknown in China.

Zheng's first voyage involved 317 ships and 28,000 people

1400

1404

The military commander **Timur** successfully reclaimed all the lands of the Mongol Empire except China, but at the cost of millions of lives. He died on his way to invade China in 1405.

1406–1420

In **Beijing**, the emperor built the Forbidden City as a winter palace. The capital of China was moved from Nanjing to Beijing in 1421.

Joan of Arc is now recognized as a patron saint of France

1424–1444

Vikings disappeared from Greenland, either leaving or dying. The cooling climate of the "Little Ice Age" perhaps made farming too difficult.

1428

The French visionary and warrior **Joan of Arc** heard voices that she believed to be divine. Following their instructions, she led French troops against the English in the Hundred Years War. She was burned as a heretic in 1431 at the age of 19.

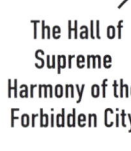

The Hall of Supreme Harmony of the Forbidden City

CONNECTING THE WORLD

1427
The Portuguese navigator Diogo de Silves first set foot on the unoccupied **Azores**, a group of islands in the Atlantic Ocean. They were well placed for ships to resupply between Africa and the Americas.

1428
Forming a "Triple Alliance" of three cities, the **Aztecs** expanded their territory in Mexico. When Aztecs conquered a city, some captives were sent to the capital Tenochtitlan for human sacrifice.

c. 1440–1450
The invention of the **printing press** in Germany changed European culture forever. It meant information could be quickly, cheaply, and widely distributed. Many more people learned to read.

1453
The Ottoman sultan Mehmed II attacked Constantinople, using cannons to blast through the city walls. The inhabitants were slaughtered or taken as enslaved persons, and the Hagia Sophia church was immediately converted to a mosque. The fall of the city marked the **end of the Eastern Roman Empire** and the final surviving link with the ancient world in Europe.

1484

1453
The Ottoman Empire closed the land route between Europe and the east, interrupting trade. This led to the search for sea routes to India and China, starting the **Age of Discovery**.

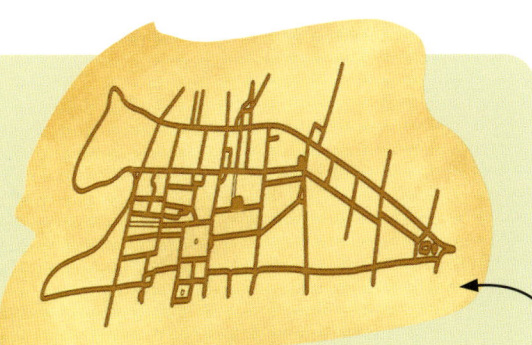

The Inca capital Cuzco was shaped like a jaguar

1438–1532
The **Incan Empire** in Peru expanded rapidly. At their height, the Inca governed 9 million–14 million people, and had both the largest empire ever seen in South America and the largest empire in the world at the time.

1482
Portuguese traders in Ghana built the first trading post, **Elmina Castle**. It later became one of the most important slave-trading stops and was used for this purpose until 1814.

CONNECTING THE WORLD

1485–1599

As the Middle Ages ended, the world became more connected. European voyages of discovery turned into quests for expansion, and the people already living in the lands the explorers came across soon suffered as a result. The people of South and Central America fell victim to European invaders first.

The Spanish invaders, or "Conquistadors," ravaged South and Central America and the Caribbean, slaughtering the local population, and destroying their cities and civilizations. They changed the ecology of the Americas and Europe by moving plants and animals between them in the so-called "Columbian Exchange." They took coffee, chocolate, potatoes, tomatoes, tobacco, and other plants to Europe, and introduced wheat, olives, grapes, horses, cattle, pigs, and chickens to the Americas.

1492
The oldest surviving **globe** was made by Martin von Behaim from Nuremberg. It excludes the Americas, Australia, and Antarctica, which were unknown to Europeans at the time.

Behaim's globe showed a single ocean (left) between Africa and Asia (right)

1485

1493
Flu first appears in the New World, followed by **smallpox** in 1507. By 1650, about 90 percent of the population had died from diseases introduced from Europe.

1492
The **Reconquista**—the taking back of Muslim Spain by Castilian Christians—was completed with the return of Granada in southern Spain.

1492
Christopher Columbus set sail from Spain, heading west. Unaware of the existence of the American continents, he hoped to reach China or India, avoiding the long and difficult journey around Africa. His three ships reached the Caribbean, where he left some settlers in Hispaniola (now Haiti).

1494
Spain and Portugal divided much of the world between them in the **Treaty of Tordesillas**. Anything "discovered" to the west of an imaginary line between the Poles belonged to Spain, and anything to the east belonged to Portugal, excluding any Christian settlements.

CONNECTING THE WORLD

1497
Vasco da Gama set sail from Portugal, looking for a sea route to India for trade with the east. After skirting the African coast, he arrived in the port of Calicut (now Kozhikode) in India, in 1498.

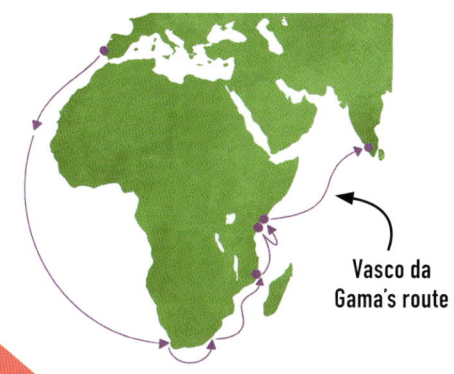
Vasco da Gama's route

1502
The **first African enslaved people** arrived in the New World, sent from Spain. Soon after, captured enslaved people were shipped directly from Africa to Spanish plantations and mines in the Caribbean.

1519
Portuguese explorer **Ferdinand Magellan** sets off to sail around the world in the service of the Spanish king. He died on the way, and only one ship of the fleet of five and 22 of the original crew of 270 returned.

1526
Babur, from Uzbekistan, conquered North India with help from the Safavid (Iranian) and Ottoman empires, founding the **Mughal dynasty**. The Mughals ruled most of India by 1707.

1543
Nicolas Copernicus published his account of the solar system, with the planets orbiting the Sun rather than Earth.

1599

Martin Luther reportedly nailed his document of complaints to the door of Wittenberg Castle Church

1517
Martin Luther, a German monk, criticized some aspects of the Catholic Church, especially letting people buy forgiveness for their sins. This started the **Reformation**, splitting the Church into Catholic and Protestant arms, and beginning a bitter struggle that dominated Europe for centuries.

1519
The Conquistador **Hernán Cortés** began his conquest of the Aztecs in Mexico, taking the city of Tenochtitlan in 1521 and becoming the first ruler of "New Spain."

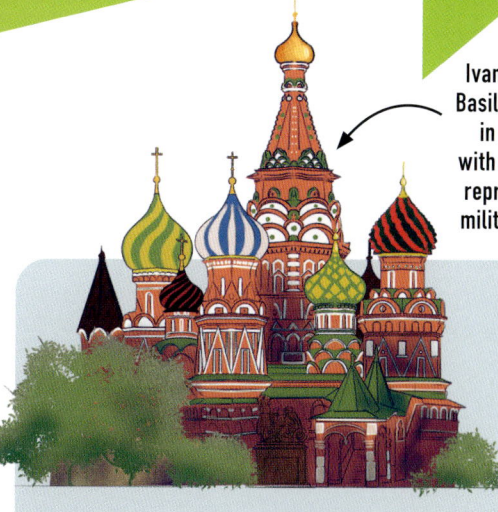
Ivan IV built St Basil's cathedral in Moscow, with each tower representing a military victory

1547
Ivan IV Vasilyevich became the first **Tsar of Russia**. In later life, he became a tyrant.

1575
Portugal founded the first **European colony in Africa**, in Angola, and began shipping enslaved people to Portuguese colonies in Brazil.

CONNECTING THE WORLD

CLOSED WORLDS

While Europeans were exploring and conquering the world, the Far East became closed and solitary. Trade with the rest of the world was cut, and over a period of several centuries China, Japan, and Korea swayed between complete isolation, with closed borders, and just limited access to foreign influences.

PIRATES AHOY!

Korea and Japan were terrorized by **wokou pirates** based around Japan from the 13th century. They attacked ships at sea and coastal settlements in Japan, Korea, and later China. Raids could involve 400 ships, and 3,000 attackers taking goods and seizing people who were sold into slavery. To avoid raiders, farming communities moved farther inland, losing good farmland. Piracy was a risky business, though—if caught, the punishment was death.

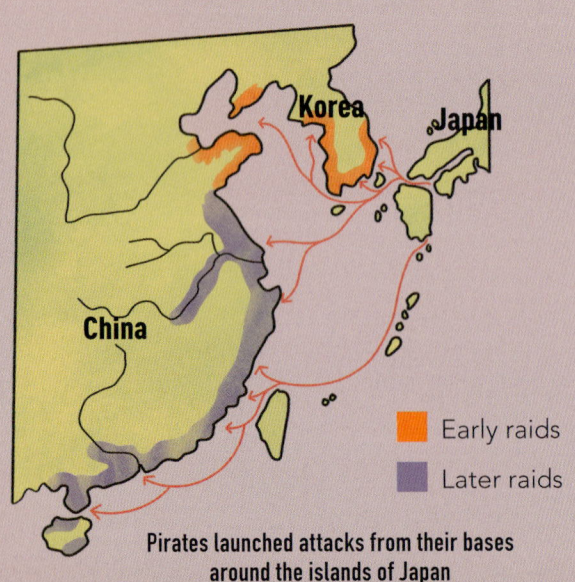

Early raids
Later raids

Pirates launched attacks from their bases around the islands of Japan

CLOSING THE DOOR

When building forts along the coast and tackling pirate ships at sea didn't work, the Chinese **banned sea trade** in 1371, and destroyed ships and dockyards starting in 1384. Any remaining ship was considered a pirate ship and could be attacked. But real traders became so desperate that piracy increased. Piracy in China only reduced after the ban on trade was lifted in 1567. Similar bans were reintroduced in the 1600s, and were more strictly enforced. Japan and Korea also took the same measure at different times, cutting off or restricting trade with the outside world. From 1633 to 1853, Japan's policy of "sakoku" ("chained country") largely restricted trade to China and Korea.

PORTUGAL IN THE EAST

The **Portuguese** were the first Europeans to enter China by sea, arriving in Guangzhou in 1517. The Portuguese were allowed to build a trading post at Macau, land that remained Portuguese from 1557 until 1999. While China was closed to trade, Macau was the only port allowing trade with Japan. Portugal dominated trade between India, Indonesia, China, and Japan.

In 1543, three Portuguese traders whose ship had been blown off course became the first Europeans in Japan, and more followed. This early Portuguese influence introduced firearms (the musket) to Japan, and allowed the entry of Jesuits (Catholic priests) who converted some Japanese people to Christianity, beginning in 1549. Portuguese traders and Jesuits were allowed to settle and trade. But with the "chained country" policy beginning in 1633, openness ended. All foreign trade went through an artificial island, **Dejima**, built in Nagasaki. No foreign traders were allowed into mainland Japan, and Christianity was banned. The Portuguese were thrown out of Dejima in 1639, and after that only Dutch traders were allowed until 1854.

The island of Dejima was just 120 m (395 ft long)

SCIENCE AND RELIGION

One of the first westerners known to learn Chinese was the Italian Jesuit **Matteo Ricci**. He was also the first to write a Chinese dictionary for western use, and the first westerner allowed into the Forbidden City in Beijing. He translated some Chinese classic texts into Latin, making a two-way intellectual exchange between Europe and China. Ricci and other Jesuits introduced both Christianity and the learning of western scientists into China. Western astronomy, in particular, was very different from Chinese astronomy, which was focused on making accurate calendars and trying to match events in the heavens to events on Earth.

CONNECTING THE WORLD

1600–1699

The 17th century was the age of growing European empires. While Spain still dominated South America, Britain took control of much of India. More British and Dutch people settled in North America, and Europeans discovered Australia.

1600

Queen Elizabeth I granted a royal charter to the **East India Company (EIC)** to trade in India on England's behalf. It was allowed to wage war to win trade and profit, and eventually had its own army. The EIC ravaged India, impoverishing its people over nearly three centuries.

1620

The **Pilgrim Fathers**, a group of 102 English Protestants, set sail from Plymouth, UK, to America on the *Mayflower*, to set up a society in "New England" based on their own interpretation of Christianity. Their religion, customs, and laws underlie much of modern America.

The Pilgrim Fathers coming to land from the *Mayflower*

1600

1601–1603

Famine in Russia killed a third of the population—around 2 million people. Crops failed after a volcanic eruption in Peru in 1600 caused cold weather around the world.

1613

Mikhail Romanov was appointed tsar of Russia, ending the turbulent "Time of Troubles"—15 years of chaos after the death of Fyodor I in 1598. The Romanovs ruled until 1917.

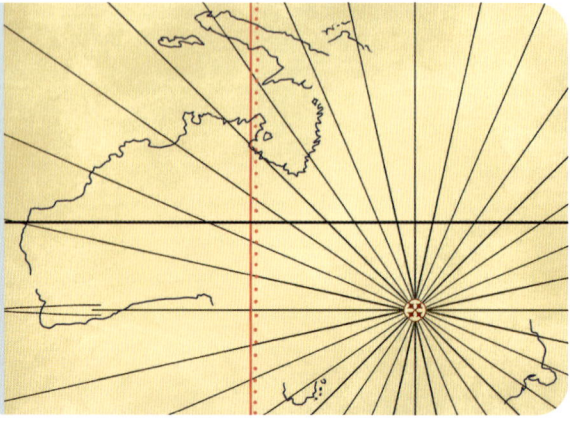

1606

The Dutch explorer **Willem Janszoon** became the first European to visit **Australia**.

Janszoon's map of the west coast of Australia

1631

Emperor Shah Jahan begins building the **Taj Mahal** in Agra, India, as a tomb and monument for his wife, Mumtaz Mahal.

CONNECTING THE WORLD

1641
Slavery was legalized in Massachusetts; other American states soon followed.

1642–1651
The **English Civil Wars** were fought between the Protestant Parliamentarians, called Roundheads, led by Oliver Cromwell, and the Catholic Cavaliers, loyal to King Charles I. The wars were a struggle to establish the balance of power between the king and parliament. The winning Roundheads executed Charles I and declared a republic under Cromwell. Oliver Cromwell died in 1658 and the monarchy was restored under Charles II (Charles I's son) in 1660. However, the monarchy now had to share power with parliament.

1645–1715
The **Maunder Minimum** was a particularly cold era of the "Little Ice Age" that affected Europe from 1300 to 1850. Intensely cold winters saw frost fairs held on rivers that now rarely freeze.

1661–1683
The **Great Clearance** in China forced people to destroy coastal property and move inland. This was to counter an anti-Qing movement based in Taiwan and supported in coastal communities. Going too near the coast was punished by death, approaching ships were destroyed, and all trade had to go through Macau. Hong Kong became a wasteland, with no inhabitants.

The ice of the River Thames in London was thick enough to support people, huts, horses, and even fires

1699

1644
The Manchu seized Beijing, ending the Ming dynasty and beginning the final imperial dynasty, the **Qing**. All men in China had to style their hair in the Manchu "queue" style, shaved at the front of the head, with a long braid behind.

Peter the Great used the title "emperor" instead of the traditional "tsar"

1687
Isaac Newton published his theory of **gravity**, which explains how planets stay in orbit around the Sun and how objects attract each other and interact gravitationally.

1682
Peter I (Peter the Great) came to the throne in Russia. He was the first tsar to leave the country, and traveled around Europe for two years, often in disguise. On his return, he remodeled the country along European lines and moved the capital to the new city of **Saint Petersburg**.

CONNECTING THE WORLD

SELLING HUMANS: SLAVERY

People have enslaved others for thousands of years. The Sumerians, Greeks, ancient Chinese, and many other early civilizations relied heavily on slavery for building, farming, and domestic work. Enslaved people often endured terrible conditions, especially in the 18th and 19th centuries.

Enslaved people were often traded at markets, and were considered the property of the person who bought them

BEING ENSLAVED

There were several ways people could become enslaved. Some may have been born into slavery, the children of an enslaved mother. Others may have been part of a group that was defeated by a conquering army. Sometimes, people who lived near a coast—anywhere from southern Ireland to China and Japan—were at risk. Pirates raided inland and snatched people who were then sold as slaves.

In the Middle Ages, the church forbade the sale of Christian slaves and so the slave trade clustered around markets in the middle east. The most extreme recent exploitation of enslaved people was the capture and sale of **Black Africans** to work in the **New World**.

OUT OF AFRICA

European invaders took land in South and North America and in the Caribbean, and began to grow crops. But a shortage of workers willing or able to do the hard work of farming in a hot environment soon led landowners into a terrible trade. From the 1570s, when Portugal opened a trading post for enslaved African people in Angola, **European colonists shipped enslaved African people across the Atlantic**. Although Arab slave traders mounted their own expeditions into Africa to capture people, European traders rarely went far inland. Instead, they bought enslaved people from African chieftains and traders. Several African kingdoms relied on the sale of their own captured enemies and rivals as a source of income.

CONNECTING THE WORLD

THE TRANSATLANTIC SLAVE TRADE

Enslaved people were chained and marched to ports, where they were packed into ships and taken over the ocean. They endured horrific conditions, treated as cargo rather than human beings. Often, between 10 and 20 percent died on the sea crossing. Once in the Americas, these people were sold to work on **plantations** growing crops such as sugar, coffee, tobacco, and cotton, or to work as **domestic servants**.

The trade made a great deal of money for the owners of ships that followed a triangular route. The ships first carried goods such as iron, cloth, and guns from Europe to Africa, where they were sold, and the hold was packed with captured people. The enslaved people were taken to the New World for sale, and the ships were restocked with items such as sugar, tobacco, and cotton to return to Europe. Few enslaved people were taken from Africa to Europe; those who did end up in Europe usually served as domestic servants and were often treated as an exotic oddity.

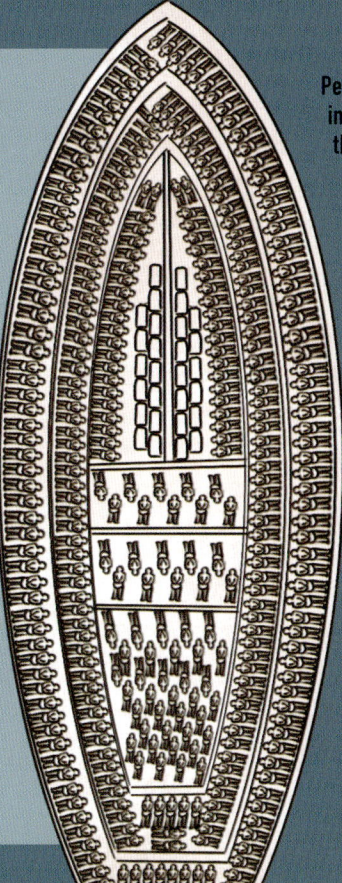

People were packed into slave ships as though they were objects

LIFE AS AN ENSLAVED PERSON

Enslaved people were considered to be **property**. They could be physically abused, shackled and chained, sold on to other owners, refused permission to marry, have their children taken away, and be treated in any other way the enslaver chose. Enslaved Africans had no rights. Many worked on plantations growing crops such as sugar and (later) cotton. The work was hard, and the enslaved people were watched over and often whipped or beaten by overseers to make sure they carried on working.

— CONNECTING THE WORLD —

1700–1799

The 18th century was a time of change, but also of troubles. In Europe, the Industrial Revolution began, changing societies forever. At the same time, Americans threw off British rule and the French overthrew their own monarchy. China and Japan still resisted involvement in the wider world.

1775–1783
The **American Revolutionary War** was fought between 13 British colonies in North America and Britain. The French joined the war in 1778, and the Americans won with their help. In 1783, America became independent.

1701
Jethro Tull invented the **mechanized seed drill**, which made planting crops much faster.

1755
The Portuguese city of **Lisbon** was destroyed by a powerful **earthquake**. It caused fires that razed the city to the ground and a tsunami that flooded the ruins. Up to 100,000 people died. It was the first earthquake studied scientifically.

1712
Thomas Newcomen developed an early **steam engine**, used mainly for pumping water out of mines.

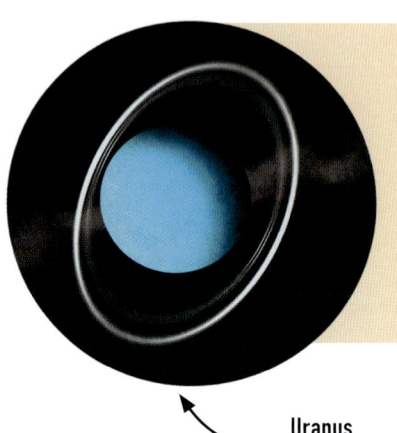
Uranus

1781
William Herschel spotted the planet **Uranus**. It was the first planet to be identified since ancient times.

1700

1757
China restricted foreign trade to the port of Guangzhou and established an area called the **Thirteen Factories**, a group of stores and warehouses that were the principal and sole legal site of most western trade with China.

1724
Peter the Great of Russia sent Danish explorer Vitus Bering to discover whether Asia was joined to America. Bering crossed Siberia to the Pacific Ocean, finding the narrow strip of sea now called the **Bering Straits** between eastern Russia and Alaska.

1762
Catherine the Great became Empress of Russia. Under her rule, Russia expanded its territory, built many new cities, and became recognized as a great power—but it still relied on serfdom (see pages 56–57).

1787
Britain began to ship convicted criminals to Australia. They became the first **European inhabitants of Australia**. The rights of the Aboriginal Australians were ignored.

Convicts arriving in Australia

80

CONNECTING THE WORLD

1789–1799
In 1789, drought, poverty, and the threat of more taxes led the common people in France to revolt against the wealthy ruling class. They formed a National Assembly to demand a new constitution (rules that say how a country is governed). Worried about the army taking over, people in Paris stormed the prison, the **Bastille**, looking for weapons and gunpowder to use to fight back. By the end of the year, the National Assembly had adopted the **Declaration of the Rights of Man**, setting out principles of equal rights.

The storming of the Bastille is often considered the start of the French Revolution

1793
The invention of the **cotton gin**, a machine to remove seeds from the fibrous "boll" of cotton, made manufacturing cotton much easier. It led to slavery expanding: As growing cotton became more profitable, many enslaved people were forced to work in the cotton fields of America.

1792
The king of France, Louis XVI, was overthrown and **France was declared a republic**.

1799

1791–1804
In Haiti, enslaved people rebelled against French rule, bringing **independence to Haiti** and abolishing slavery by 1794.

General Toussaint Louverture led the slave rebellion that became a war of independence in Haiti

1793–1794
With in-fighting between the revolutionaries, the **French Revolution** descended into a bloodbath, called the "Reign of Terror." The king was executed in 1793, and anyone accused of opposing the revolution, including most of the rich, were also executed. Eventually, the people rebelled against the violence and a more moderate government took over.

Many French aristocrats were executed using the guillotine

1799
The army general **Napoleon Bonaparte** seized power in France, ending the Revolution.

CONNECTING THE WORLD

INDUSTRIAL REVOLUTION

While revolutions in France, Haiti, America, and South America changed the lives of people in those places, the Industrial Revolution eventually changed the whole world. Beginning in Britain around 1750, it produced the modern world of mechanized and industrialized production of goods on a large scale.

STARTING WITH FUEL

At first, water power was used to drive machinery, and the main fuel used was **wood**. But as more forests were cut down, wood became expensive. **Coal** became a more important fuel. The Industrial Revolution was possible in Britain because it had large natural deposits of coal.

In 1712, Thomas Newcomen invented a coal-powered **steam engine**. This could pump water from coal mines, making mining much more efficient. Steam engines were used to mine coal, which was used to power more steam engines! But steam engines could also be used to power other types of machinery. When James Watt improved the steam engine in the 1760s, its use in manufacturing really took off, starting with fabric-making.

James Watt's steam engine

FROM MINE TO FACTORY

Steam engines changed **transport** as well as the manufacturing industry. The first trains, in Wales in 1804, were used to move iron and coal from mines, but soon began moving other goods and people around. Steam engines were also used for boats and ships—and eventually a similar principle was used to make cars.

The DeWitt Clinton locomotive first ran in America in 1831

FROM FARM TO FACTORY

Children were often employed to drag trucks of coal in the mines, as they could fit through low, narrow tunnels deep underground

Before the Industrial Revolution, around 80 percent of the world's population worked farming food; today, around 1 or 2 percent of people in industrialized nations work in farming. Improvements in technology and better farming practices meant that more food could be produced more easily, with fewer workers. Many people who had worked in farming were forced to look for other work. Some went to work in the expanding coal mines; others moved into the cities, where the **factories** needed workers. But the new work was often performed in terrible conditions.

CONNECTING THE WORLD

MINING ORES

The demand for coal meant more people had to work in the mines. But mining was not only for coal. The demand for **iron** to make machinery and other metals and chemicals used in industrial processes meant there was more mining of many types. The metal needed was then extracted from the ore and cast into metal objects in **foundries**. Here, people worked in intense heat with very dangerous molten metal.

FABRIC FIRST

One of the most important products of the Industrial Revolution was **cloth**. Spinning yarn and weaving were once time-consuming processes, but mechanization made them quick. Huge factory looms produced wool and cotton fabric quickly. **Cotton** was in particular demand. It had been imported from India, where low wages made producing cotton fabric cheap. But new factories made cheap manufacture possible in Britain. Cotton was grown in America by enslaved people, and was shipped to Britain for automated weaving. Working in the factories among huge, fast-moving machinery was dangerous and unpleasant.

UNHEALTHY LIVES

People worked long hours in harsh and dangerous conditions, and lived crowded together in sprawling **slums** of very poor-quality homes with little fresh air or space. The air in and around cities was polluted with smoke and fumes from the factories, the rivers were polluted with industrial waste, and many people suffered from bad health as a result. Wages were low, and people, including children, had to work many hours a day. Most children started work by the age of 10.

CONNECTING THE WORLD

1800–1849

The first half of the 19th century saw drastic changes in Europe that ended with revolution (see page 86). Napoleon rose to power and then fell, while Britain began a long process of abolishing slavery. It was a time, too, of famine and disaster.

1804
Napoleon was declared Emperor of France. Prior to this, he had already begun a series of military campaigns, attacking other European countries and invading Egypt.

1808–1825
After Napoleon's troops overthrew the king of Spain, the **Spanish states in South America** became independent due to this and other causes.

1815
The volcano **Tambora** erupted in Indonesia, the largest eruption in nearly 2,000 years.

1800

1804
Meriwether Lewis and William Clark set off to **explore** the interior and west of **North America**. They covered 12,870 km (8,000 miles) and reached the Pacific coast.

1807
The **Slave Trade Act** made transatlantic slave trading **illegal** in the British Empire. It was not a requirement that existing slaves had to be freed.

1812
Napoleon invaded Russia, but his army was not equipped for the Russian winter, and most soldiers died of cold, exhaustion, or disease. Only 10,000 of 600,000 men returned in fair condition. It was the beginning of the end for Napoleon, who died in exile on St Helena, a tiny island in the Atlantic Ocean, in 1821.

1816
Shaka became the chieftain of the small Zulu tribe in South Africa. A military genius, he soon conquered many other tribes. It is said by some that, driven mad by grief after his mother's death, he executed hundreds of people and banned the planting of crops or use of milk. He was assassinated in 1828.

CONNECTING THE WORLD

Volcanic dust in the sky caused dramatic sunsets and sunrises for years

1816
The **year without a summer** followed the eruption of Tambora. Dust and ash blocked sunlight, causing cold weather and crop failures globally. The resulting famines killed at least 100,000 people.

1838
British troops entered **Afghanistan**, capturing the capital, Kabul, the year after. Britain was expanding its empire in Asia, but Russia also wanted to control the land. The invasion began the **Great Game**—a series of confrontations that continued into the 20th century.

1845–1852
The **Irish Potato Famine**, caused by an infection that destroyed the potato crop, killed around a million people. Farmers depended on potatoes for both money and food. Ireland was ruled as a British colony at the time, but Britain did nothing to help.

1820
The continent of **Antarctica** was first seen by a Russian expedition.

1849

1819
In Britain, new **laws banned children under nine working**, and limited those aged 9–16 to working fewer than 12 hours a day.

Before the new laws, children as young as four worked up to 14 hours a day as "scavengers," collecting scrap cotton beneath working mills

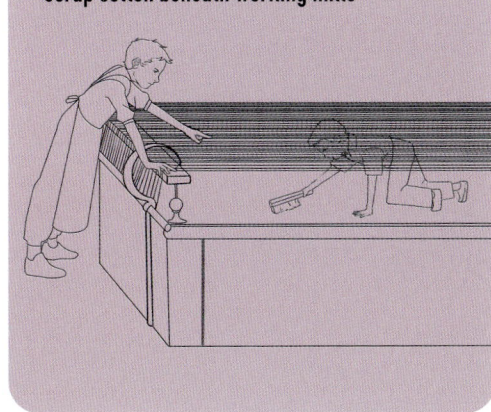

1831
Cyrus McCormick demonstrated the first commercially successful **combine harvester**, which helped revolutionize farming practices.

1833
The **Slavery Abolition Act** abolished slavery in most British colonies. There were exceptions, including areas held by the East India Company.

1839–1842
The **First Opium War** was fought to stop Britain smuggling the addictive drug opium into China. Opium was illegal in China, but quickly became popular. After losing two Opium Wars, China was forced to legalize opium, open more ports, and grant Hong Kong to Britain.

1845
In North America, the concept of **manifest destiny** was used to justify forcing Indigenous peoples from their land. The doctrine claims that America has a divine right to expand across the continent.

1848
The Communist Manifesto by Karl Marx and Friedrich Engels claimed that the "means of production" should be owned by the workers, and resources should be distributed according to need. They hoped workers would unite and overthrow the ruling classes.

CONNECTING THE WORLD

YEAR OF REVOLUTIONS

In 1848, Europe erupted into revolution. From Romania in the east to France in the west, Sicily in the south and Poland in the north, people rose up against political systems that seemed outdated and unfair. It was the most widespread wave of revolution Europe has ever seen.

LIGHTING THE FIRE

The systems of government that had worked in Europe for centuries didn't suit the new world of the **Industrial Revolution**. Many people had moved from farms into cities, where their work was hard and dangerous, and their homes unhealthy. In both towns and countryside, people suffered as a result of mechanization, forcing them out of their traditional jobs and into low-grade, underpaid work. Talk of **freedom** and **reform** was in the air: about the abolition of slavery, women's constrained lives, and the dire state of the poor. Bad harvests in the 1840s brought matters to a head. All around Europe, people wanted more rights and better government.

Paris was one of the first cities to erupt into revolution in February 1848

ALL FOR ONE

Many modern European countries were not single nation-states in 1848. Germany was a collection of states, of which Prussia was the largest. Italy was divided into several small states with different rulers. On the other hand, Austria-Hungary was a large empire that covered not just Austria and Hungary, but also several other central and eastern European countries. In many parts of Europe, the struggles of 1848 developed into **struggles for nationhood**, whether that was uniting small states or escaping the rule of a larger empire.

In Berlin and other German cities, revolutionaries demanded German unification

In the streets of European cities, revolutionaries fought from behind street barricades

MICRO TIMELINE

1847–1848: In Sicily, women rioted at bread prices; Sicily overthrew its French overlords.

February 1848: Revolution in Paris and other French cities. The people sent the king and parliament into exile, and appointed a new government, electing Louis Napoleon (grandson of Napoleon Bonaparte) as president.

March 1848: Revolutionaries in Germany called for the unification of the German states into a single country, freedom of the press, and freedom of association (freedom to meet and share ideas).

March 1848: Uprisings in Austro-Hungary overthrew the unpopular leader, Metternich. Once he was gone, rich and poor turned against each other as the wealthy didn't want to give working people rights.

March 1848–August 1849: The revolution in Hungary lasted the longest. Although finally crushed by the Russian tsar Nicholas I helping Austro-Hungary, it successfully ended feudalism there.

■ Revolutionary uprising
■ German confederation

Armies sometimes used cannons against the under-equipped revolutionaries

YEAR'S END

The ruling classes had been taken by surprise, and the revolutionaries won early success in most places. But as the wealthy regrouped, they quashed the revolutions in the summer of 1849 and reasserted their power. The revolutionaries lacked organization and often contained groups with conflicting ideas and aims: The wealthier middle classes didn't want to give rights and power to the poor. Near normality was restored by 1851, although some places had changed forever.

One of the most important outcomes was that in many places **feudalism finally ended**, and people working the land gained some control of their lives. France never had another king, and remained a republic. Italy and Germany were set on the path to unification (becoming single nation-states). Some despised rulers had been removed for good. And a seed had been sown. The **rights** people were fighting for—freedom of the press, the right to vote whether or not they owned property, greater rights over their own lives—have since been won in Europe.

CHAPTER 5

THE WORLD AT WAR

The century between 1850 and 1950 saw the world transformed. Many things became truly global, including war and disease. Humans reached both the North and the South Poles for the first time. European invaders made further inroads into Africa and divided the continent between them. White Americans pressed farther west, driving out and abusing the Indigenous peoples. They changed the landscape, killing the herds of bison that previously roamed the plains and tearing up the prairie grass to plant farm crops.

With much of the world under European rule, when war broke out in Europe in 1914, and again in 1939, it soon escalated into World Wars that drew in people from colonies. War was a spur to developing new technology. The First World War saw tanks and planes used; the Second World War brought nuclear weapons and rocket-powered bombs—but it also brought new medicines with antibiotics, first used to treat soldiers.

THE WORLD AT WAR

1850–1899

The second half of the 19th century saw rising nationalism—nations becoming more concerned with growing their own power and influence, protecting their own people, and cooperating less with other countries. In France and Russia, rulers focused on industrialization and modernizing. In China and India, people resented rule by foreign powers.

1850–1864
In the **Taiping Rebellion**, the religious leader Hong Xiuqian and 2 million followers tried to overthrow the Qing dynasty in China. They were unsuccessful, but the rebellion killed at least 20 million people.

1857–1859
Indian soldiers rebelled against the British East India Company (BEIC) over the use of animal fat in weapons. Britain put down the rebellion, then dissolved the BEIC to rule India directly as a colony.

1859
Charles Darwin published his theory of **evolution**, explaining how organisms change over time. Many people objected to the idea that humans are just another evolved animal, rather than being specially created by God.

1863–1864
The International Committee of the Red Cross (ICRC) was founded in 1863. A year later, in 1864, the First Geneva Convention was set up in response to the atrocities witnessed in 1859 during the catastrophically violent **Battle of Solferino** between France, Piedmont (in Italy), and Austria-Hungary.

1850

1853
Dutch painter **Vincent van Gogh** was born. He went on to produce some of the world's most famous paintings, such as *The Starry Night* (1889) and his *Sunflowers* series (1888–1889), before he died in 1890.

1851
The **Great Exhibition** was organized at the specially built Crystal Palace in London, England, to showcase "Works of Industry of All Nations." In fact, more than half of the 100,000 exhibits were products of the British Empire. It was the first and most successful of a series of international "world fairs," with 6 million visitors.

1860–1861
The revolutionary **Giuseppe Garibaldi** led a movement to unify Italy. The Kingdom of Italy was declared in 1861, and unification was completed in 1871 with the capture of Rome.

THE WORLD AT WAR

1861
Realizing Russia had to modernize and industrialize to catch up with Europe and the USA, **Tsar Alexander II** freed 20 million serfs. He also reorganized the army, planned railroads around the vast country, changed the legal system, and sold Alaska to the USA for $7.2 million.

Serfdom in Russia survived for centuries after it was abolished in most of Europe.

1869
The **Suez Canal** was completed in Egypt, joining the Mediterranean and the Red Sea, and dividing Europe and Asia.

1869
People in the west first heard of the Chinese **giant panda** when a hunter sent a panda skin to a French missionary.

1899

The American Civil War was mostly a dispute about slavery. The northern states had industrialized, while the southern states still relied on farming using enslaved people. In 1860, when the anti-slavery president Abraham Lincoln was elected, the southern states separated and formed the Confederate States of America. It was the first war to use iron-clad warships and railroads, and to be photographed. With the defeat of the southern states, the USA abolished slavery.

1861–1865
The **American Civil War** raged between the northern and southern states, killing up to 2 percent of the population.

1870–1871
After a successful war against France under the leadership of **Otto von Bismarck**, Germany was unified with Wilhelm I as emperor.

1885
The **first car** was produced by Karl Benz in Germany. It used a petrol-driven internal combustion engine.

The first car had only three wheels.

THE WORLD AT WAR

THE INVASION OF AFRICA

While European powers had been active in East Asia for a long time and the British Empire controlled India, Africa was largely unexplored by Europeans. The Portuguese, British, and French had set up trading posts around the coast, but most trade was carried out with Africans who went inland bringing metals, ivory, and enslaved people to trade. As some nations banned the slave trade, colonial powers looked for other ways to make money from Africa. This would be disastrous for Africa and Africans.

A HOSTILE ENVIRONMENT

Europeans going inland to the "interior" of Africa faced problems and often died. Tropical diseases, hostile Africans defending their land and goods, and shortages of food and drink killed many. In 1876, the Belgian king Leopold II set up the **International African Association** to research the continent and find out what lay inland. The researchers found that there were rich natural resources including gold, copper, diamonds, and rubber.

The tropical disease malaria, carried by mosquitoes, killed many Europeans who went to Africa.

CARVING UP THE CONTINENT

Once Europeans knew of Africa's natural wealth, they became eager to take it. At a conference in Berlin in 1884, 12 European states, the Ottoman (Turkish) Empire, and the USA divided up the continent between them in the **Scramble for Africa**. No representatives of African nations were present. The Europeans treated Africa as available to be divided in whatever way they agreed—and then set off to claim their lands. Before the Berlin conference, 10 percent of Africa was under European rule, but by 1914 that had risen to nearly 90 percent.

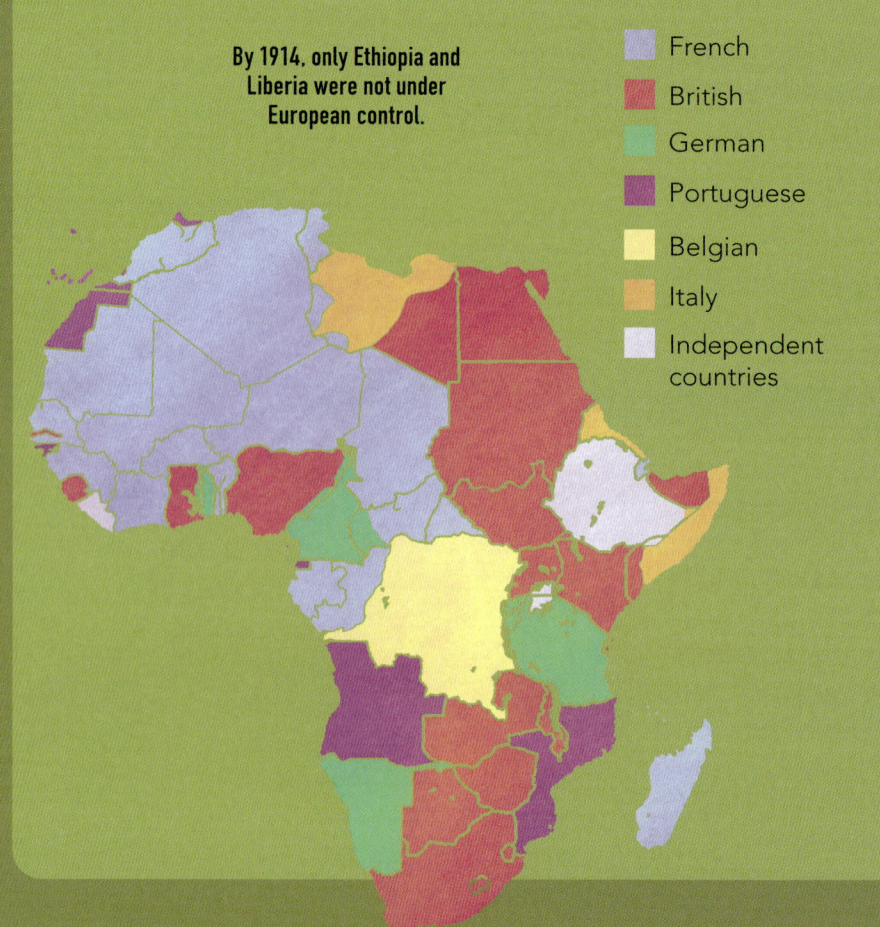

By 1914, only Ethiopia and Liberia were not under European control.

- French
- British
- German
- Portuguese
- Belgian
- Italy
- Independent countries

DOMINATING AFRICA

The colonial powers forced their own ideas and ways of life on the people in the countries they took over. Many people were forced to speak the language of the invaders, such as English or French, and these are still official languages in many parts of Africa. European education systems and styles of government were forced on African people, and their original systems disappeared along with some of their languages. The worst impact, though, was on individuals. Many died of diseases brought in by Europeans. Many were forced to work for the invaders for low pay, were ill-treated or killed, and had their land and possessions stolen. The **Herero people** of German South West Africa (Namibia) rebelled against the German colonists taking their land and cattle. Their uprising was crushed, and the Herero people were slaughtered, or imprisoned at the Shark Island concentration camp in 1904.

Herero prisoners

WAR WITH TECHNOLOGY

Modern technology helped Europeans to take Africa. The invaders produced maps of the regions they traveled through, and laid **railroads** to gain access to the interior. The landscape of forest, mountains, and desert made travel difficult, and building railroads was the most effective way of linking the interior to the coast. Europeans built railroads in Africa in order to move troops around (to secure and maintain territories), to move mined metals, and to move crops from productive farming areas. All goods had to be transported to the coast for an onward journey by ship.

THE WORLD AT WAR

SUFFRAGE

In a democracy, the people can vote for representatives who set the laws and govern for them. Although the earliest democracy was in Greece more than 2,000 years ago, only men were allowed to vote in elections until recently. Women's battle for the vote, or for "suffrage," was a long and bitter struggle fought around the world. The latest state to allow women to vote was Saudi Arabia in 2015.

EARLY VOICES

Some people started campaigning for **women to have the vote** from the 18th century. In fact, the state of New Jersey in America granted the vote to White women who owned property in 1776—but then took it away again. In Sweden, women could vote from 1718 to 1772. Female chieftains of the Iroquois tribe in North America are recorded as being able to vote in 1654, and perhaps many other groups that have not left written records also allowed women to play a part in government. Through Europe and North America, women began to campaign vigorously in the later 1800s for the right to vote.

PROTEST AND PUNISHMENT

In some countries, particularly in Britain, there was a split between women who would go on peaceful protests and more militant campaigners who would disrupt events and damage property. Emmeline Pankhurst led the breakaway group, the Women's Social and Political Union, in 1903. They called themselves **suffragettes**, while the more law-abiding group were **suffragists**. Many of these more militant protesters were arrested and imprisoned.

THE WORLD AT WAR

NOT ALL WOMEN (OR MEN) ARE EQUAL

Today, modern democracies allow all people above a certain age to vote. In the past, before women could even vote at all, men could often only vote if they **owned property** or were of a **certain social class**. When countries such as Britain and the USA introduced votes for women, they first started with women who owned property. The voting age for women was generally older than that for men. In Australia, women who owned property could vote in local elections from 1864. When a new law was passed in 1902 allowing more women to vote in national elections, Indigenous women were excluded.

In prison, many women went on **hunger strike**, refusing to eat. They were force-fed, a cruel process that involved pushing a tube down the throat to pour food directly into the stomach. This was intended to break the woman's spirit, and often caused real physical harm. From 1913, women in danger of death from hunger strike and force-feeding were released from prison until their health recovered. Then they were taken back in, and the process continued.

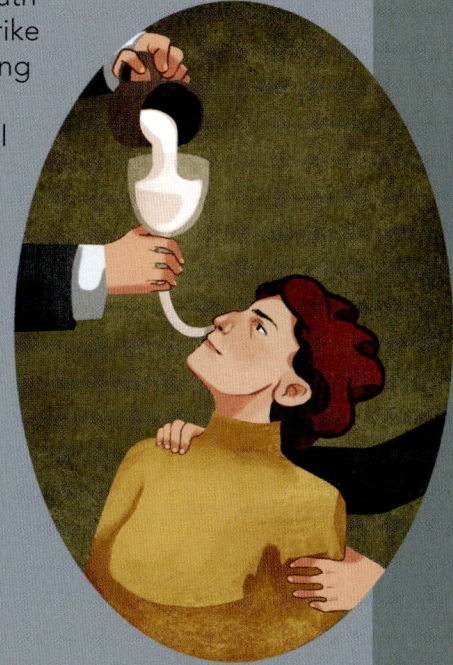

EQUALITY AT LAST

In the USA, the first national march for women's suffrage took place in 1913 in Washington. Although women had been campaigning for the vote since 1848, only four states allowed women to vote in state elections, and that hadn't changed since 1896. Led by Alice Paul, American women wanted women throughout the USA to have voting rights. The **constitution was changed** in 1920, but it took decades before all women, and particularly Black women, were able to vote. In Britain, women over 30 were allowed to vote from 1918. Ten years later, the age was dropped to 21, the same as for men.

THE WORLD AT WAR

1900–1919

The start of the 20th century was marked by upheaval. There was conflict between and within nations, with unrest, revolution, and outright war. The 1910s ended in the cataclysm of the First World War and a global pandemic, which between them claimed up to 100 million lives when the world population was only around 1.6 billion.

1901
Six British colonies came together to form the **Commonwealth of Australia**.

1908
A mysterious explosion in the air over a forest in Tunguska, Russia, flattened 80 million trees. It was probably an **exploding asteroid**.

1911
The Norwegian explorer **Roald Amundsen** was the first person to reach the South Pole.

1900

1905
Riots, strikes, and protests ended in **revolution in Russia**, where most of the population lived in terrible conditions. Tsar Nicholas II was forced to give up absolute power and create a parliament (called the "Duma").

1906
A devastating **earthquake** followed by fires destroyed the city of **San Francisco**, USA.

1910–1920
The **Mexican Revolution** overthrew the president. Revolutionaries turned against each other, assassinating leaders one after another, and the revolution lasted at least 10 years.

1911
An army uprising overthrew the Qing dynasty in China, ending 2,132 years of imperial rule. The **Republic of China** was announced in 1912, with Sun Yixian (Sun Yat-sen) as president. The Chinese Nationalist Party formed with the aim of reunifying China.

1910
The first airships, called **Zeppelins** after their inventor, carried paying passengers. This was the only way people could pay to fly at the time. The first commercial plane flight came in 1914.

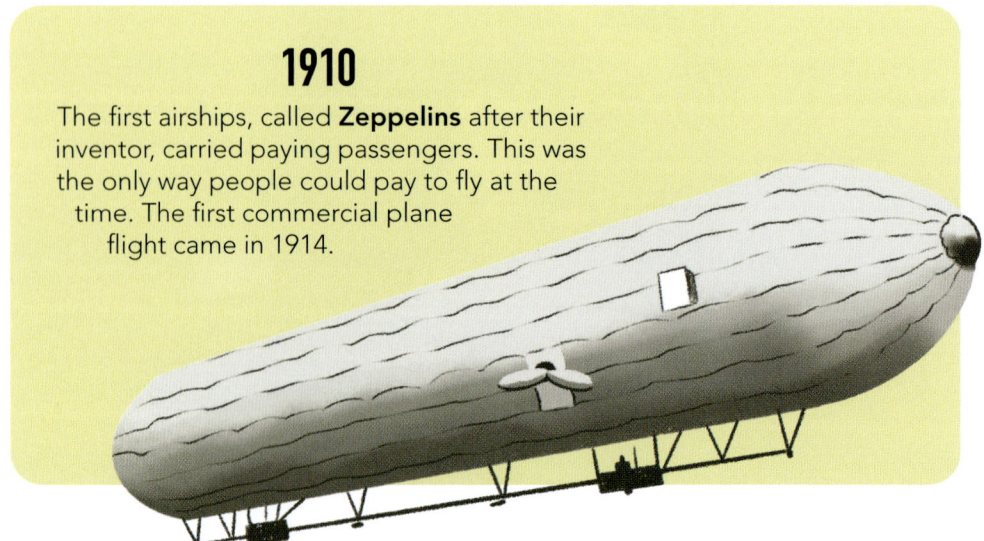

THE WORLD AT WAR

1912
The largest ship ever built, the **RMS Titanic**, hit an iceberg in the North Atlantic Ocean on the way to New York and sank, killing more than 1,500 people. Changes in shipping safety followed the disaster.

Titanic had been considered unsinkable

1915–1917
The Ottoman Empire in Turkey killed many **Armenians** and drove others from their land in an act of genocide. Between 600,000 and 1.5 million Armenians died. The Islamic government feared the Christian Armenians would betray Turkey in the First World War.

1917
Two revolutions in Russia in a single year overthrew Tsar Nicholas II and produced the world's first **communist state**.

Industrialization drove poor Russian peasants into cities to find work, where they suffered desperate living conditions. Russia had been hit hard by famines, defeat in two wars, and the 1905 revolution, and entering the First World War was disastrous. The February Revolution forced the tsar to abdicate. A new government brought welcome reforms, but kept Russia in the war, which was unpopular. The October Revolution overthrew the new government and put the Bolsheviks in power under Vladimir Lenin to build a communist state.

1919

1914
The **Panama Canal** was completed, joining the Atlantic and Pacific Oceans through Panama in Central America.

1918–1922
The **Red Terror** was a period of persecution and violence in Russia following an attempt to assassinate Lenin. The secret police targeted everyone seen as an enemy. Around 100,000 people were killed, and more were put in prison camps, tortured, and used as forced workers.

1914–1918
Archduke Franz Ferdinand, heir to the Austro-Hungarian empire, was assassinated in Sarajevo, Bosnia, triggering the **First World War** (see pages 98–99).

1918–1919
A **pandemic of flu** spread around the world. With no treatments or vaccines available, at least 50 million people died, devastating nations already hit hard by the First World War.

THE FIRST WORLD WAR

The First World War didn't come as a surprise. Tension had been building for a long time. The countries of Europe had made treaties (agreements) to support one another if they were attacked, and many had been growing their armies and stores of weapons. The Triple Entente (France, Russia, and Britain) were on one side, and the Triple Alliance (Germany, Austria-Hungary, and Italy) on the other. It was a tense time that took only a small trigger to plunge the continent—and then the world—into the most devastating war there had ever been.

FROM ONE DEATH TO MILLIONS

Archduke **Franz Ferdinand** was assassinated in 1914 by a Serbian group working to free Bosnia from rule by Austria-Hungary. A few days later, Austria-Hungary declared war on Serbia. Russia opposed Austria-Hungary, and the powers of the Triple Alliance and Triple Entente soon followed into the war. The Turkish Ottoman Empire joined on the side of the Triple Alliance. The war lasted until 1918, and around **20 million people died**.

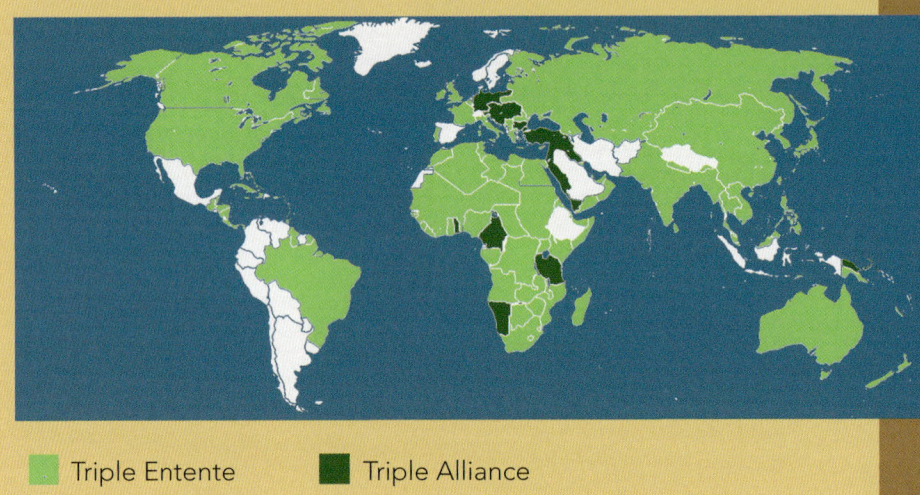

■ Triple Entente   ■ Triple Alliance

INTO THE TRENCHES

Germany planned first to defeat France on its western frontier, and then attack Russia. It wasn't that easy. War with France soon turned into slow battles fought from **trenches** dug through the fields of Belgium and France. Hundreds of thousands of soldiers lived and died in appalling conditions, and the surrounding countryside and villages were destroyed.

THE WORLD AT WAR

COLONIES AND BEYOND

Many European nations had **colonies** in other parts of the world, and these were **drawn into the conflict**. New Zealand (British) invaded Samoa (German), and Australia (British) attacked New Guinea (German). Japan declared war on Germany and Austria-Hungary, and attacked German ports in China. Colonies in Africa fought on the sides of their colonial overlords. The British Army in India, larger than the British army itself, fought for Britain. Battlefronts extended around Asia and Africa as well as Europe. In the seas, ships of opposing sides attacked one another. Ships and submarines also fought to stop the transport of troops and delivery of essential items, including food and weapons.

THE LAST "OLD" WAR

The First World War saw the transformation from old-style war to more **modern war**. It was the last war to have large cavalry units (soldiers on horseback) and to use cannons. It was the first war to use fighter planes, machine guns, barbed wire, and poisoned gas.

German U-boats were armed submarines that targeted military and merchant shipping

AN END TO THE "WAR TO END ALL WARS"

Countries entered and left the war. Russia withdrew after its second revolution in 1917. Romania left soon after. America entered the war as a response to German attacks on American shipping, part of Germany's plan to starve Britain by cutting off supplies. In 1918, German troops were pushed back, and it became clear they were losing. Unrest in Germany turned into revolution. In November, the kaiser (king) abdicated and the war was over in days. In 1919, the Weimar Republic was declared, with a government made up of a president, chancellor, and parliament. A **treaty** drawn up at **Versailles**, France, imposed harsh punishment on Germany, including huge compensation payments and a ban on having an army.

The German, Austro-Hungarian, Ottoman, and Russian empires all fell, borders were redrawn in Europe, new republics were founded, and some nations were re-established as independent states.

THE WORLD AT WAR

1920–1939

The 1920s and 30s were a challenging time. Societies reeled in the aftermath of the First World War and the global flu pandemic, stricken by grief and poverty. A significant proportion of the world's young men were dead or injured. In Europe, the harsh conditions of the peace imposed on Germany led toward the Second World War.

1924
On the death of Lenin, **Joseph Stalin** took over the USSR.

1921
The **Chinese Communist Party** was formed, with help from the Communist Party of the USSR.

1922
The bloody civil war that began with the Russian revolutions of 1917 ended with the foundation of the **Union of Soviet Socialist Republics (USSR)**. It was a one-party state, with the ruling Bolsheviks becoming the Communist Party under Lenin.

1923–1938
Mustafa Kemal Atatürk became president of the new **Turkish Republic**. He focused on westernizing and secularizing Turkey, reducing the influence of Islam.

1927–1949
Civil war in China pitted the government against the Communist Party. The war paused in 1937–1945 while China fought off an attack by Japan and the Second World War raged.

1920

1922
A team led by English archaeologist Howard Carter found the tomb of the boy-pharaoh **Tutankhamen** in Egypt, buried under the sand for 3,000 years.

Howard Carter also found other objects in the tomb, including Tutankhamen's iron dagger.

1923
A period of **hyperinflation** made money worthless in Germany. The crisis resulted from war debts paid to France and Belgium. The government printed more money, but price rises got out of hand—the price of a loaf of bread rose from 250 marks to 200 billion marks in 10 months. Many people lost everything they had.

1929
Stalin introduced **collectivization**. Farmland was seized from farmers and organized into government-owned collectives. People who opposed the move were killed or imprisoned.

German banknotes were worth so little that people used them as wallpaper. A new currency was issued to rebalance the economy, and old notes were burned.

THE WORLD AT WAR

1929–1939
Economic problems in the USA led to the **Wall Street Crash** in 1929, when the value of stocks and shares plunged. The **Great Depression** followed—a period of economic collapse and businesses failing. With a quarter of the workforce unemployed, people queued for food at street soup kitchens.

Destitute Americans lived in makeshift homes made of iron sheeting and scraps in shanty towns

1934–1940
A mix of bad farming practices and drought led to **dust bowl** conditions in the central USA. The soil was blown away by heavy winds, stripping the land and making farming impossible. The storms led to the **Great Migration** as 2.5 million desperate farming people moved, looking for work and better living conditions.

The choking winds of the "dust bowl" killed people and cattle

1930
Under Mahatma Gandhi and Jawaharlal Nehru, the **Indian National Congress** declared its aim to achieve India's total indepedence from British rule.

1932–1933
Famine swept Ukraine and the USSR, the result of failed collectivization. In Urkaine, nearly 4 million people starved—around 13 percent of the population.

1939

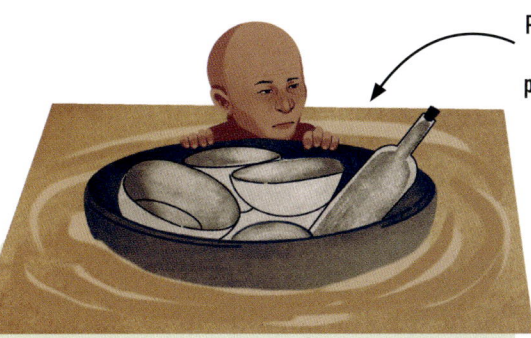

People struggled to save themselves and their possessions from muddy flood water

1931
Floods around the Grand Canal and the Yangtze, Yellow, and Huai Rivers in China were the worst natural disaster ever, with around 2 million people killed. Most of central China was under water.

1933
Adolf Hitler was appointed Chancellor of Germany and the next year was elected President, too. Wanting to make Germany a one-party state, he began to expand the state police and stamp out opposition.

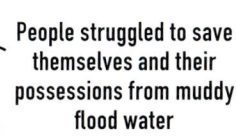

1936–1938
The **Great Terror** in the USSR under Stalin was a purge of anyone suspected of anti-Soviet ideas. More than 700,000 people died, many by execution.

1939
The **Second World War** started after Germany invaded Poland.

THE WORLD AT WAR

THE SECOND WORLD WAR

After the First World War and the hard times that followed, many people in Europe became nationalists—they had a fierce sense of national identity and wanted their own country to succeed. This was especially true in Germany, which suffered a great deal after the First World War. Nationalism led directly to the Second World War, which had the highest death toll of any war ever: more than 50 million people died, over half of them from the USSR.

READY FOR WAR

Hardship in Germany enabled the Nazi ("Nationalsozialismus") leader **Hitler** to rise to power. He offered the German people hope of being proud of their nation again, but their trust was misplaced. Hitler wanted to engineer a "master race" of Germans and to build an empire (or "Reich") that would last for 1,000 years. He began by persecuting Jewish people, destroying their businesses, and removing their rights. He took over Austria and part of Czechoslovakia for Germany. In 1939, he invaded part of Poland. Other European nations had put up with Hitler until this point, a policy called "appeasement," but would not tolerate him invading other European countries. Britain and France declared war on Germany. In 1940, Germany invaded France and Belgium, and despite British help, France was overcome and had to surrender.

Jewish people in areas occupied by Germany were forced to wear a special badge identifying them as Jews. This made it easy to persecute them.

WAR FROM THE AIR

The Second World War was the first major war in which **planes** were very important. Hitler planned to invade Britain and tried to defeat the British air force first with a battle in the air, but Britain won. Then German planes bombed London and other British cities in an attack known as the **Blitz**. Aerial bombing of cities remained an important strand of the war and killed thousands of civilians. British forces also fire-bombed German cities, reducing some historic cities to ashes.

During the Blitz, people living in London sheltered from the bombs in Tube (metro) stations

Bombed cities often burned for days. The fire-bombing of Dresden in Germany was a humanitarian catastrophe.

THE WORLD AT WAR

TECHNOLOGY OF WAR

Both sides raced to develop new and more powerful weapons. Germany was the first to get **rocket-powered bombs**, as rockets had already been in development before the war. Planes improved on both sides. The most devastating technology developed for the war was the **atomic bomb**, made in the USA. This harnessed atomic power for the first time, breaking atoms apart to release a devastating blast of energy.

Many women worked in ammunitions factories, making bombs

THE WORLD FIGHTS

As in the First World War, the war spread beyond Europe. European nations with empires called on their colonies for troops. Colonies were attacked and blockaded by the enemy to disrupt shipping lines bringing essential food, troops, and other supplies. Japan entered the war on the side of Germany, and attacked China and British colonies in East Asia. An attack by Japanese planes on **Pearl Harbor**, where American war ships were docked, brought the USA into the war in 1941. Disruption to shipping threatened food supplies, and people in some European countries suddenly had to grow far more of their own food.

ANNIHILATION

In his drive for racially "pure" Germans, Hitler aimed to wipe out Jewish people and other groups, including people with disabilities and Roma people. They were sent to **concentration camps** in Germany and Poland, where many were murdered immediately and others were worked to death. When the camps were opened by British and American soldiers at the end of the war, the full horror of what had happened there was revealed.

Auschwitz concentration camp

THE WORLD AT WAR

1940–1949

The Second World War and its aftermath dominated the 1940s. After the war, the European colonial empires began to break up, with countries becoming independent again. An uneasy alliance had existed between the west (Europe and the USA) and the USSR during the War, but it became increasingly tense.

1940

The **Battle for France** began after Germany invaded France, Belgium, and the Netherlands. France surrendered to Germany, and its government was replaced with a new one that cooperated with the Nazis.

1941–1944

Germany attacked the USSR. The army surrounded **Leningrad** (now Saint Petersburg), stopping the movement of supplies, including food, into the city. At 872 days, it was one of the longest sieges in history. Hitler aimed to destroy the city and its people entirely.

Up to 1.5 million people died in the siege of Leningrad, many of starvation

1945

Japan surrendered, ending the war in Asia, after the USA dropped atomic bombs on **Hiroshima** and **Nagasaki**. The bombs caused devastation, flattening the cities, killing at least 120,000 people and horribly injuring others. Many more died later from burns and exposure to radiation.

1940

1940–1941

Germany began the **Blitz**, an intense bombing campaign against cities in Britain, killing 40,000 people.

1942–1943

One of the longest, deadliest battles in history was fought between Germany and the USSR at **Stalingrad** (now Volgograd). Around 2 million people died or were injured. Germany's defeat at Stalingrad was a turning point in the war.

1945

As Soviet troops marched into Berlin, Hitler killed himself and **Germany surrendered**, ending the war in Europe.

1945

The **United Nations (UN)** was founded to protect peace, defend the rights of all people, and promote the success and prosperity of all humankind. In 1948, it set out the rights that should be respected everywhere in the Universal Declaration of Human Rights.

1945

With Japan's defeat in the Second World War, **Taiwan** (under Japanese control since 1895) was occupied by China for the Allied forces. It became an independent republic in 1949.

Most bombing in the Blitz was at nighttime

THE WORLD AT WAR

1945
Civil war broke out in **China**, the Kuomintang under Chiang Kai-shek fighting the Chinese Communist Party under Mao Zedong.

1948
Israel was founded as a Jewish homeland in part of **Palestine**, a Muslim Arab country previously governed by Britain. The 1948 Arab–Israeli War broke out immediately, as adjacent Arab states objected to giving Muslim land to the Jewish people.

1945–1948
Stalin undermined elections to install communist governments in Albania, Bulgaria, East Germany, Romania, Poland, Hungary, and Czechoslovakia. He wanted them as a buffer zone between the USSR and western Europe, fearing the west would attack the USSR.

1948
The segregation of Black and White people in South Africa, called **apartheid**, began to be strictly enforced.

1948
In England, the **National Health Service (NHS)** was founded—the world's first free-at-point-of-use health service, funded by taxation.

1949

Mahatma Gandhi led the movement for Indian independence, but was assassinated the year after it was achieved

1947
India won independence from Britain and split into **India** and **Pakistan**. Pakistan became a largely Muslim country, while India was home to Sikhs and Hindus. Violence and turmoil followed as people moved around. Many people lost everything they had as they fled religious persecution.

Mao began a series of reforms that changed China utterly

1949
The communists won the civil war in China. **Mao Zedong** declared the People's Republic of China with himself as Chairman. Chiang Kai-shek fled to Taiwan.

1949
The **North Atlantic Treaty Organization (NATO)** was set up to defend the west against the USSR, which was seen as a threat.

THE WORLD AT WAR

TYRANTS AND DICTATORS

The 20th century saw several oppressive, and often brutal, governments in Europe, Asia, South America, and parts of Africa. These were generally under the control of a dictator—a ruler who had seized power or extended his power beyond the level that the country's constitution (rules of government) generally allowed. When a dictator stoops to abuse of their power and commits atrocities against their own people, they become a tyrant.

LEFT AND RIGHT ALIKE

Dictators can be politically right-wing or left-wing. Although they may come from different starting points, their extreme positions often end up looking very similar: oppressing the people, using violence, secret police forces, and persecuting anyone they see as opponents. As they have absolute power, their ideas and actions aren't softened by the advice of others.

Tyrants make a lot of enemies, and many are assassinated or overthrown. Fear of this often drives them to obsessively hunt out and destroy opponents.

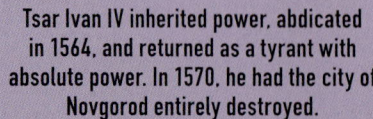

Tsar Ivan IV inherited power, abdicated in 1564, and returned as a tyrant with absolute power. In 1570, he had the city of Novgorod entirely destroyed.

THE ROAD TO POWER

Dictators and tyrants come to power by different routes. Some rise through military force or revolutions. Others begin by inheriting power or winning an election, but then extend their power illegally.

Tyrants of the 20th century include Stalin in the USSR, Adolf Hitler in Germany, Mao Zedong in China, Idi Amin in Uganda, Pol Pot in Cambodia, Franco in Spain, Augusto Pinochet in Chile, and Kim Jung Il in North Korea.

Stalin came to power peacefully after the death of Lenin. Like many dictators, he held **rigged elections** so that he appeared to hold power legally.

Mao Zedong was the leader of a revolutionary army that won the Chinese civil war. Pol Pot was a revolutionary who won over the peasantry of Cambodia, then attacked and defeated the unpopular government in 1974.

Stalin ruled the USSR unopposed for almost 30 years

THE WORLD AT WAR

Idi Amin

An **army** can be a threat to any leader, as it has people and weapons. General Francisco Franco in Spain and General Augusto Pinochet in Chile both used armies they commanded to seize power. Franco led rebel troops in Spain's civil war in the 1930s, while Pinochet led a coup to overthrow the elected president Salvador Allende, who had appointed him general of the Chilean army. In 1971, Idi Amin overthrew the president, Milton Obote, while head of the army in Uganda.

IDEOLOGIES AND PERSONALITIES

Some dictators have powerful (though misguided) **beliefs in ideas** that direct what they do. Hitler believed in the superiority of the German people, and that Germany could and should be the greatest power in Europe. Mao Zedong and Pol Pot pushed communist ideologies, regardless of the suffering and death they caused.

Others focus on their own **desire for power**. Amin and Pinochet killed thousands whom they saw as threats to their power. Kim Il Sung, ruler of North Korea 1948–1994, built a personality cult around himself. People who did not sufficiently revere him were often killed or imprisoned. He divided citizens into "core," "wavering," or "hostile," depending on how loyal to him they were. This categorization affected all aspects of their life, including the work they could do, how much food they had, and where they could live.

Kim Il Sung

KEEPING CONTROL

Tyrants rely on a vicious **secret police force** and encouraging people to betray each other. In Stalin's USSR, anyone suspected of opposing the communists was sent to a "gulag," a prison camp in freezing Siberia where they were kept in terrible conditions and forced to work, often to death. In Chile, Pinochet used the army to find opponents who were then imprisoned, tortured, or killed.

Political prisoners were forced to do back-breaking work despite being severely malnourished

107

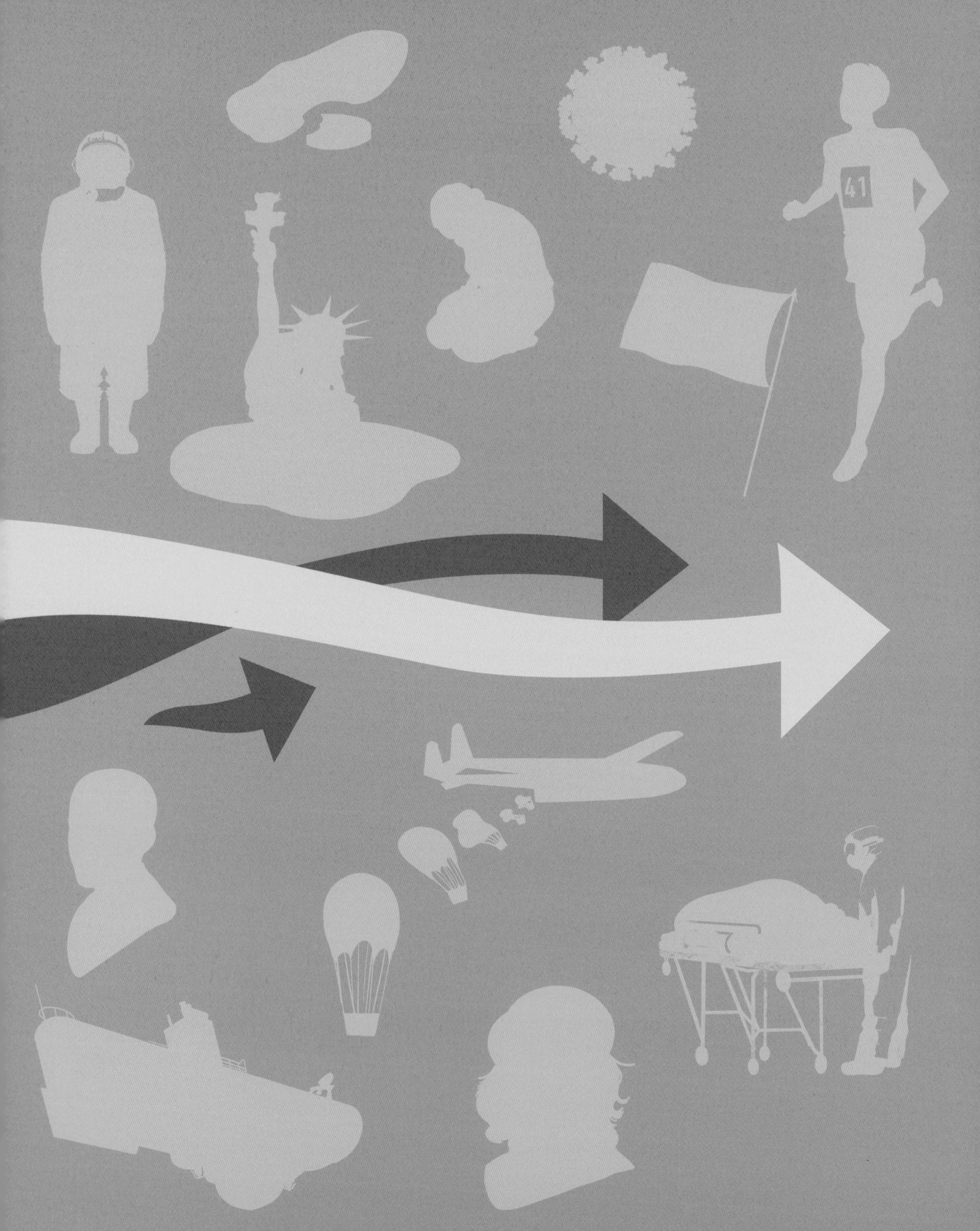

CHAPTER 6

THE MODERN WORLD

After the Second World War, the modern world began to take shape. Some countries that had become newly independent struggled to find their way at first. Many were poor, having lost their resources to colonial powers in the 18th and 19th centuries. For the second half of the 20th century, too, the world was roughly divided by the Cold War into communist and capitalist powers, each feeling threatened by the other. The opposition between communist and western states decreased with the fall of the USSR, but new tensions emerged, particularly between some Arab Muslim countries and the west. The end of the 20th century saw a new kind of global cooperation through trade that has been called globalization. The production of food and goods is spread around the world, and some commercial businesses have become as large and powerful as some nations. But this has brought its own problems, and nationalism—a focus on national pride rather than international cooperation—has grown in the 21st century.

THE MODERN WORLD

1950–1964

Tension between east and west, communist and capitalist states, turned into real fighting in Vietnam and hotspots in Europe and Cuba. The USA had its own problems, stemming from the continuing mistreatment of Black people, while China suffered under Mao's rule.

1950

The USSR and the People's Republic of China (PRC) sign a Treaty of Friendship, Alliance, and Mutual Assistance. Several governments around the world, including the UK government, officially **recognize the PRC**.

1954

The British athlete Roger Bannister became the first person to **run a mile (1.6 km) in under four minutes**.

1955

The **Warsaw Pact** was a defence treaty between the Soviet Union and seven other communist states in central and eastern Europe: Albania, Bulgaria, Czechoslovakia, East Germany, Hungary, Poland, and Romania. It was signed after (then) West Germany joined the western NATO alliance, to try to balance NATO power.

1955–1975

The **Vietnam War** raged between communist North Vietnam and South Vietnam. South Vietnam was supported by the USA with its policy to fight communism anywhere it arose. The war was long and difficult, with many atrocities committed against civilians (non-soldiers). It became increasingly unpopular in the USA, and they withdrew from it in 1973. The war ended in 1976, with Vietnam unified as the Socialist Republic of Vietnam.

1950

1953

The mountaineers Edmund Hillary from New Zealand and Tenzing Norgay from Nepal became the first people to climb **Mount Everest**, the highest mountain in the world.

1955–1968

The fight for equality by Black people in the USA began as a grassroots movement after a Black woman, **Rosa Parks**, was arrested for refusing to give up her seat in a White-only section of a bus.

The civil rights movement fought for the rights of Black American citizens. In the 1950s, Black people often had to use different facilities from White people, and had fewer rights. They couldn't travel on the same buses, use the same schools, or often even live in the same areas. The civil rights movement used both violent and peaceful protests as it campaigned for equal and fair treatment.

1957

The first satellite, **Sputnik 1**, was launched into space by the USSR, starting the "space race" between the USSR and USA (see pages 116–117).

Sputnik 1, just 56 cm (22 in) across, sent simple radio signals to Earth for several weeks

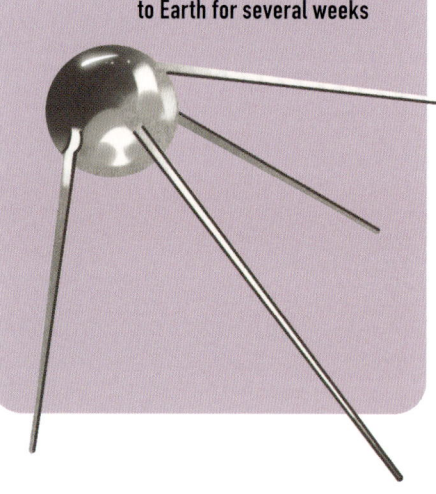

THE MODERN WORLD

1958–1962
Mao Zedong introduced the **Great Leap Forward**, a policy intended to modernize China's industry and agriculture and solidify Chinese communism. It was a terrible failure, leading to the deadliest famine in history, killing 15–55 million people in 1959–1961.

1960s–1994
In South Africa, 3.5 million Black people were forcibly removed from their land into areas known as **Bantu homelands**, where they were plunged into poverty. Their farms were sold cheaply to White farmers.

The Trieste was crewed by Don Walsh and Jacques Piccard.

1960
The first crewed vehicle reached the bottom of the **Mariana Trench** in the Pacific Ocean, the deepest part of Earth's seas, at 11 km (7 miles) deep.

1962
The **Cuban Missile Crisis** brought Earth close to full-scale nuclear war (see page 113).

1964

1959
Revolutionaries **Che Guevara** and **Fidel Castro** overthrew the government of Cuba. The previous government, led by General Batista, had the support of the USA. The new government began a nationalization programme, and the USA responded with a trade embargo (a refusal to do trade). Cuba then appealed, successfully, to the USSR for support.

1960
The **Valdivia earthquake** in Chile was the most powerful ever recorded.

1961
Russian cosmonaut Yuri Gagarin became the **first human in space** in a small space capsule called Vostok 1.

THE MODERN WORLD

THE COLD WAR

Although Britain, France, and the USA had fought alongside the USSR in the Second World War, they trusted each other less and less in the following years. This led to the Cold War, a time of open hostility between them. At times, the Cold War was in danger of turning into a real—and probably nuclear—war. It ended in 1991 with the collapse of the USSR.

COMMUNISM VERSUS CAPITALISM

At the heart of the Cold War was a **conflict of ideology**. The communists supported a strong central government and communal ownership of land, factories, and public goods. The Communist Party was always in power, and there were no democratic elections. Communist societies were heavily policed, with brutal punishments for anyone who opposed the state. The western capitalist countries supported personal and economic freedom. People chose their government in democratic elections, and were generally free to discuss politics without fear of a secret police force. Private ownership of businesses, land, and public goods produced both opportunity and social inequality.

The conflict between east and west was played out on the world stage. In 1950, communist North Korea invaded South Korea in the hope of unifying the country. South Korea resisted, and the USA entered the war to defend South Korea against attack by the communists. It was the first armed conflict of the Cold War.

Each side distrusted the other, and spying was big business. This shoe has a hidden radio transmitter for a spy to use to send messages secretly.

BLOCKING BERLIN

After the Second World War, **Europe split into east and west**, with the east under communist rule. Germany was split into East and West parts and the capital city, Berlin, was also split into East and West, although it was in the area controlled by the USSR. Stalin worried that the west would try to seize East Germany. In 1948, he cut all land routes into West Berlin, starting a blockade that lasted 11 months. West Berlin soon ran short of food, medicines, fuel, and other essentials. The allies (Britain, France, and the USA) air-dropped supplies to West Berlin until Stalin lifted the blockade in 1949. The Berlin blockade was the start of the Cold War.

Essential supplies were dropped by planes into West Berlin

THE MODERN WORLD

EUROPE DIVIDED

Fiercely guarded borders divided east and west Europe, and citizens of the east weren't allowed to move to the west. The division of east and west became most visible in 1961, when the USSR ordered the East German communist government to build the **Berlin Wall**, separating East and West Berlin. The Wall cruelly divided friends and family, since East Germans weren't allowed to cross it.

People peered through gaps in the Berlin Wall to see friends on the other side—or just to see what was going on

Nuclear bunkers, hidden behind huge metal doors, were vast underground living spaces with supplies for many people

WAITING FOR WAR

East and west both stockpiled weapons and raced to produce more and more powerful bombs. Both sides tried out their deadly atomic weapons in tests, displaying their strength. They built **nuclear bunkers** where people could shelter if nuclear war happened. Much of this was just for show: Nuclear war between the two superpowers would have devastated the world, and nuclear bunkers would have been of little use.

TIPPING POINT

The most critical moment of the Cold War came in 1961. The USA tried to prompt an uprising against the communists in Fidel Castro's Cuba, but failed. In response, the USSR moved **nuclear missiles to Cuba**, aimed at the USA. After a tense few days of negotiation in 1962, the USSR agreed to remove its missiles, and the USA agreed to remove its own missiles from Turkey. War was narrowly avoided.

THE MODERN WORLD

1965–1974

The 1960s were a time of hope and social change in parts of the west, but of further hardship for people living under communism in the USSR and China. Black Americans gained rights, pressure to end the Vietnam War mounted in the USA, and the space race ended with two American astronauts setting foot on the Moon.

1965
Muslim Black civil rights leader **Malcolm X** was **assassinated** in the USA.

1967–1974
Three **Greek army generals** overthrew the Greek king and government in 1967. A military council called a **junta** then ruled the country, imprisoning and torturing anyone considered to have communist leanings or who spoke against the ruling military. The monarchy was abolished in 1973. A failed attempt by the junta to depose the president of nearby Cyprus led to its collapse. Democratic elections were held in 1974.

1968
The **Prague Spring** was an attempt to soften communist rule in Czechoslovakia. Alexander Dubček replaced the unpopular and severe communist leader Antonín Novotný and tried to introduce reforms such as freedom of speech and a better standard of living. After four months, the USSR sent tanks and thousands of soldiers to Prague, the capital, and removed Dubček. The country returned to repressive communist rule.

1965

1966–1976
Mao Zedong launched the **Cultural Revolution**, hoping to revive the revolutionary spirit in China and purge the country of anti-revolutionary ideas. Political enemies of Mao were jailed or killed, as were many intellectuals whose ideas were considered hostile to the Communist Party, including students, doctors, writers, and artists. Many were sent to work on communal farms. Around 1.5 million died and 20 million were sent away from their homes.

1968
A **flu pandemic** starting in Hong Kong or China killed 1–4 million people worldwide.

1968
An expedition led by the American Ralph Plaisted was the first to reach the **North Pole** using snowmobiles. The next year, the first expedition on foot arrived at the Pole.

1968
Christian Black civil rights activist **Martin Luther King** was **assassinated** in the USA. King promoted peaceful protest, and this approach was openly opposed by some activists. His death sparked riots and outrage, but civil rights laws were soon passed in the aftermath.

THE MODERN WORLD

1969
Apollo 11 **landed on the Moon** with two American astronauts.

1972
Members of the Palestinian Liberation Organization (PLO) **took Israeli athletes hostage** at the Olympic Games in Munich, Germany, demanding the release of Palestinian prisoners. The hostages and some terrorists were killed in a rescue attempt.

This was the first terrorist attack broadcast on live TV

When the state of Israel was created in 1947, many Jewish people moved there, wanting to escape to the safety of a homeland after persecution under the Nazis. The Palestinians whose land had been taken to make Israel, and nearby Arab Muslim states, opposed the reallocation of Palestinian land. The PLO and Israeli state fought each other—a conflict that continues today.

1974

The Bhola cyclone was one of the deadliest in history

1969
The first **single-chip microprocessor**, the Intel 4004, packed computing power onto a tiny sliver of silicon. It played a crucial role in the development of personal computers.

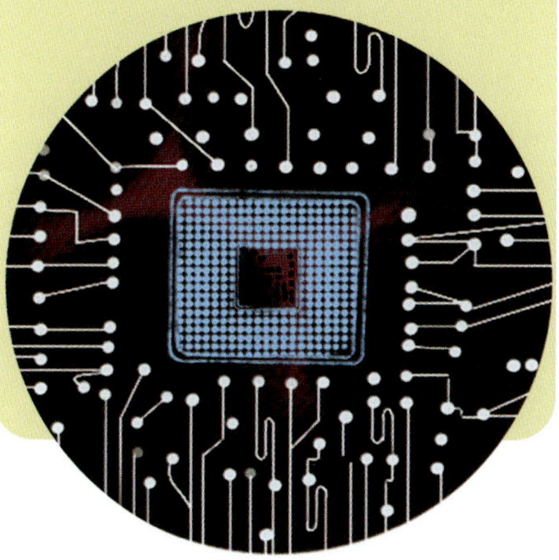

1970
The **Bhola cyclone** hit Bangladesh (then part of Pakistan), killing as many as 500,000 people.

1973–1990
With the support of the USA, **General Augusto Pinochet** overthrew the elected socialist government to become dictator of Chile. His rule was marked by the murder, imprisonment, and torture of opponents and innocent citizens. Around 80,000 people were arrested and many simply disappeared, never to be seen again.

THE MODERN WORLD

THE SPACE RACE

The Cold War wasn't only about spying, military hostility, and disliking the other side's politics. There was competition in all areas, including sports, technology, and space exploration. The "space race" was the race between the USSR and the USA to get into space. The USSR was in the lead at first, but the USA claimed victory by putting humans on the Moon in 1969.

OFF THE GROUND

The first **rockets** were made in Germany in the 1920s. They were soon adapted as bombs in the Second World War, and their use as spacecraft was put on hold until later. In 1947, scientists in America sent fruit flies and seeds into space to test the effect of cosmic rays on them, and during the 1940s and 50s both the USA and USSR sent unfortunate monkeys, mice, and dogs into space, most of which died. These rocket trips were up and then down, just entering space and returning, but in 1957 the USSR used a rocket to launch the first satellite, Sputnik. It stayed in orbit for several weeks.

THE MOON AND BEYOND

The American president, J.F. Kennedy, was determined that America should not fall behind in the space race. In 1961, he announced that Americans would **land on the Moon** before the end of the decade. The American Apollo program first sent spacecraft to the Moon with no crew, then took humans around the Moon, and finally landed in July 1969.

A huge rocket launched each Apollo craft, but only a tiny top portion traveled to the Moon

PEOPLE IN SPACE

The USSR was first to get a **man into space** (Yuri Gagarin in 1961) and then a **woman** (Valentina Tereshkova in 1963). Indeed, although American Alan Shepard visited space in 1961, it took more than 20 years for an American woman to follow—Sally Ride in 1983. In 1965, the USSR achieved another first when Alexei Leonov left his craft and floated in space for 12 minutes—called a "space walk."

Valentina Tereshkova

THE MODERN WORLD

By sending humans and robots into space and building space stations, we have found out much more about the universe

Lunokhod 1 rover

Voskhod 2 spacecraft

Luna 1 orbiter

Salyut 1 space station

Venera 4 was a probe sent to explore Venus

While reaching the Moon was a major focus, it wasn't the only aim of the space race. Soviet craft were sent to **Venus** and **Mars**, but with a high failure rate. The first "soft" (non-crash) landing on Venus was in 1970. The Soviet Venera craft were the first to enter the atmosphere of another planet, the first to land successfully on another planet, and the first to record sounds on another planet. The first Soviet landing on Mars in 1971 was only briefly successful. The USA had more success; in 1965, Mariner 4 sent back the first close-up photos of the Martian surface.

AT HOME IN SPACE

Both the USA and the USSR wanted a permanent base in space, and both set out to build **space stations**. The first success was the USSR's Salyut station, which started operating in 1971. The first US space station, Skylab, was operational from 1973. On a space station, astronauts can carry out experiments and conduct space walks using a suitable spacesuit.

The space race ended in 1975 when astronauts from the USSR and USA met in space. An Apollo and a Soyuz spacecraft docked in space and the two commanders, Thomas Stafford and Alexei Leonov, shook hands.

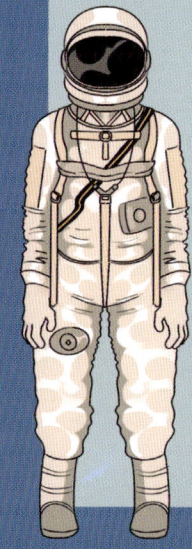

USA

USSR

THE MODERN WORLD

1975–1989

The 1970s were dominated by the Cold War, but this eased toward the end of the 1980s. At the very end of the decade, the eastern countries of Europe began to abandon communism. The USSR struggled to compete with the west and to give its people an adequate standard of living—a struggle it was about to lose.

1979

The **USSR invaded Afghanistan** after an anti-communist leader, Hafizullah Amin, overthrew the unpopular communist government that had seized power in 1978. The USSR killed Amin, but couldn't defeat the guerrilla fighters. They pulled out of Afghanistan in 1989.

1975–1979

The extremist group the **Khmer Rouge took over Cambodia** under the leadership of Pol Pot. They killed "intellectuals"—even including people who just wore glasses or spoke two languages. Everyone was moved out of cities into the countryside where Pol Pot tried to create a communist society that had no money or religion, and all property was held by the government. Up to 2 million people died of disease, starvation, exhaustion through forced work, or execution.

1980

The communist group Shining Path started a "People's War" of **guerrilla attacks and terrorism in Peru**. It took over much of the countryside and was effective until its leader, Abimael Guzmán, was captured in 1992.

1975

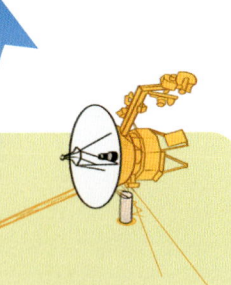

1977

The USA launched two **Voyager spacecraft** to travel past several planets and then leave the solar system. They're still going, traveling into interstellar space.

1979

A revolution in Iran installed **Ayatollah Khomeini** as head of an Islamist state. The revolution was originally supported by groups with widely differing ideas. The new government soon adopted strict Islamic law and dropped former supporters. People with more liberal ideas were persecuted.

1981

The USA launched the space shuttle **Columbia**, the first fully reusable spacecraft. It launched into space as a rocket, but landed like a plane.

1985

Newly-elected leader of the USSR, Mikhail Gorbachev, adopted radical new policies of **perestroika** (economic restructuring) and later **glasnost** (openness) in a move to modernize the USSR, ease relations with the west, and improve living conditions. Gorbachev reduced Soviet interference in eastern Europe and made treaties with the west.

THE MODERN WORLD

1986
A disastrous accident blew apart one of the four nuclear power reactors at the **Chernobyl** nuclear power plant in Ukraine (then in the USSR). Radioactive material contaminated the local area and drifted across Europe. The area around Chernobyl is still a no-go area.

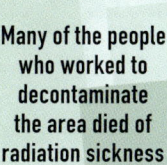

Many of the people who worked to decontaminate the area died of radiation sickness

1989
Peaceful protests against the Chinese Communist Party were brutally put down by tanks in **Tiananmen Square**, Beijing. The protests, which were started by students but grew to over a million people around the country, demanded freedom of speech and democracy. Troops fired on the crowds, probably killing thousands.

1989

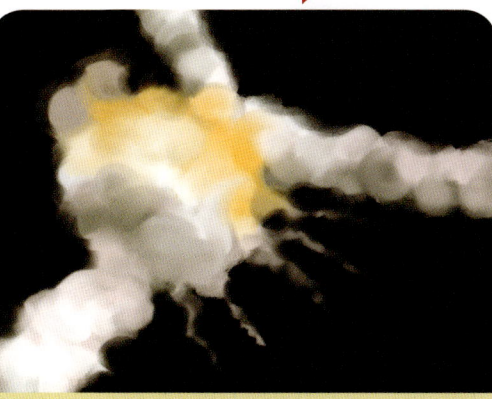

1986
The American **Challenger** space shuttle **exploded** just after take-off.

1989
The oil tanker *Exxon Valdez* struck a reef and spilled about 50 million litres (13,208,602 gallons) of crude oil into the sea near Alaska. It contaminated 2,100 km (1,300 miles) of coastline, killing thousands of sea creatures and an estimated 250,000 birds.

1989–1991
Revolutions in eastern Europe ended communist rule in Europe. Poland, Hungary, Romania, Czechoslovakia, East Germany, and Bulgaria all established new governments. The **Berlin Wall** was **torn down** by the citizens of Berlin, paving the way for the reunification of Germany.

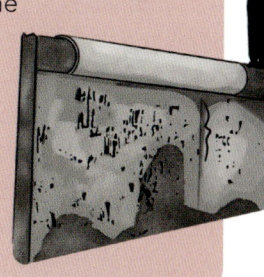

THE MODERN WORLD

1990–2004

The changes that the 1990s brought were so great that one American author even wrote that people were seeing the "end of history"—that humankind and society had achieved their final form. It wasn't the case. But the end of the Cold War and the birth of the World Wide Web did transform the world.

1991 ONWARDS

Boris Yeltsin became president of Russia. Together with some other ex-Soviet republics like Ukraine, Georgia and Belarus, Russia formed the **Commonwealth of Independent States** (CIS). In Russia, Yeltsin's reforms in the 1990s allowed freedom of the press and western-style market forces, but resulted in widespread corruption and crime, with a few very rich and many very poor people. In 1999, Yeltsin handed over to Vladimir Putin. Ukraine and Georgia would later leave the CIS.

1990–1991

The USSR began to break up, as member states like Latvia and Estonia tried to declare independence. After a failed coup (rebellion) against him, in late 1991, President Gorbachev officially dissolved the USSR and resigned.

1993

CERN put the **World Wide Web** software in the public domain. It has revolutionized how people communicate, work, share knowledge, and even socialize.

1990

1990–1994

A transitional period lasting several years led to the **end of apartheid** in South Africa.

Under the South African legal system, called apartheid, people were treated differently according to their race. Power rested in the hands of the minority White population. The African National Congress (ANC), which campaigned against apartheid, was banned in 1960 and its leaders arrested. National and international opposition grew, and in 1990, a new president, F. W. de Klerk, freed political prisoners, lifted the ban on the ANC, and allowed freedom of the press.

The ANC leader Nelson Mandela was freed from prison in 1990

1994

The first free vote in South Africa elected **Nelson Mandela** as the first Black president.

1994

In the African state of Rwanda, extremists in the majority Hutu ethnic group massacred an estimated 800,000 people from the minority Tutsi group in an atrocity known as the **Rwandan genocide**.

THE MODERN WORLD

1994–1998
Famine killed up to 3.5 million of the 22 million people living in **North Korea** after floods destroyed harvests, grain stores, and infrastructure.

2001
Terrorists hijack four passenger planes, crashing two into the twin towers of the **World Trade Centre** in New York, and another into the **Pentagon**, the USA's military headquarters in Washington, killing nearly 3,000 people. It was the deadliest attack ever on USA soil. The Islamist extremist group **al-Qaeda** staged the attacks, led by Osama bin Laden, who blamed the USA for war in the Muslim Arab world.

The attack became known as "9/11" because it happened on September 11

2001
The USA urged allies to join it in a **"war on terror"**—a global attempt to destroy terrorist organizations. The first step was bombing Afghanistan and overthrowing the Taliban (the Muslim government of Afghanistan that helped al-Qaeda). In 2002, Hamid Karzai was chosen to head the government by representatives from 364 districts of Afghanistan.

1995
After communist Yugoslavia started to break apart and **civil war erupted** between its three main ethnic groups (Serbs, Croats, and Bosnians), around 8,000 Muslim Bosnians were murdered by Bosnian Serb soldiers at Srebrenica. A United Nations peacekeeping force failed to stop this massacre, the largest in Europe since the Second World War.

1997
The American rover Sojourner **landed on Mars**. Sojourner was the first spacecraft to move over the surface of another planet.

2003
As part of the "war on terror," the USA and allies **invaded Iraq** and captured Iraqi leader Saddam Hussein.

1997
Great Britain returned Hong Kong to China after 99 years of rule. China promised that Hong Kong could keep its capitalist system and have more political freedom than is allowed in the rest of China.

2002
The USA opened a detention camp at **Guantanamo Bay**, Cuba, to hold prisoners captured in the "war on terror." It became very controversial, because people were held there for a long time without trial, and there were accusations some were tortured.

2004
An **earthquake and tsunami** in the Indian Ocean killed at least 225,000 people in several countries (including Indonesia, Sri Lanka, and India) in just a few hours.

THE MODERN WORLD

2005–PRESENT

The early 21st century saw increasing conflict between the west and the Muslim Arab world. At the same time, smart phones, social media, and other aspects of online communication changed how people lived and related to each other. The early effects of climate change, a global pandemic, and widespread economic problems added to a general sense of gloom.

2005
The **Kyoto protocol** came into force, a global agreement to limit the rise in temperatures caused by greenhouse gases. The first five-year period, 2008–2012, aimed to reduce emissions to 5 percent below the level in 1990. Instead, they rose.

2007–2008
A **global financial crash** plunged people into poverty and ruined businesses and banks. Banks in the USA had lent money to people who couldn't afford to pay it back, then sold the loans on to investors for more than they were worth. The US housing market collapsed, and the mismanaged financial markets followed.

2009
A massive **dust cloud** 500 km (310 miles) wide and 1,000 km (620 miles) long spread across **eastern Australia**. It dumped red dust and dirt over cities, disrupted transport, and harmed people with lung conditions and breathing difficulties.

2005

2006
Saddam Hussein, previously president of Iraq, was **executed** for war crimes and crimes against humanity.

2007
The first **iPhone** was released. "Smart" phones gave users full access to the internet and the ability to take photos and videos, revolutionizing personal communications.

2008
Barack Obama was elected as the first Black president of the USA.

2011
The strongest **earthquake** ever recorded in Japan led to a tsunami that damaged a nuclear power station at **Fukushima**, causing a radiation leak as serious as the Chernobyl incident of 1986.

2011
Osama bin Laden, founder and leader of the terrorist organization al-Qaeda, was **killed** by US troops. Bin Laden had started al-Qaeda to wage *jihad* (a holy war) against the west, and particularly the USA, in the hopes of establishing a global Islamic empire.

THE MODERN WORLD

2013
China launched its **Belt and Road initiative**, a 21st-century counterpart to the Silk Routes. It planned a "belt" of overland routes and a "road" of sea routes joining China to Africa and Europe for trading.

2015
IS destroyed 20–30 percent of the ancient city of **Palmyra** in Syria which was more than 4,000 years old, and beheaded the caretaker of the city.

2017
A total solar eclipse is visible in some parts of the USA. This rare astronomical event happens when the Sun, Moon, and Earth line up perfectly so the Moon completely blocks out sunlight, casting part of the Earth's surface into shadow, and revealing the Sun's outer atmosphere, called a corona. Scientists study this corona to learn more about the Sun, as well as the effect the eclipse has on Earth's atmosphere and wildlife.

2014
The terrorist organization **IS (Islamic State)** wanted to create a worldwide extreme Islamic state. IS grew rapidly. Its actions were extremely brutal, and it posted videos of its atrocities online.

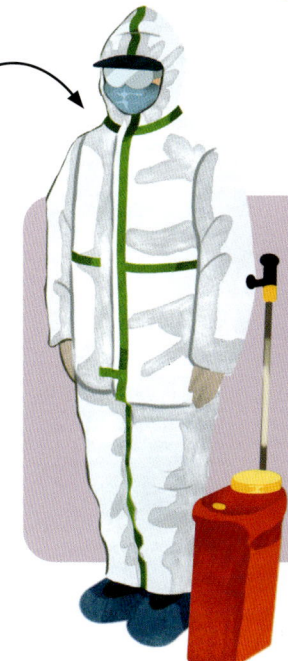

Public health workers in China tried to stop the spread of COVID-19 by spraying disinfectant in the streets

2019
A new strain of respiratory disease emerged in Wuhan, China late in 2019. Named **COVID-19**, it developed into a worldwide pandemic in 2020.

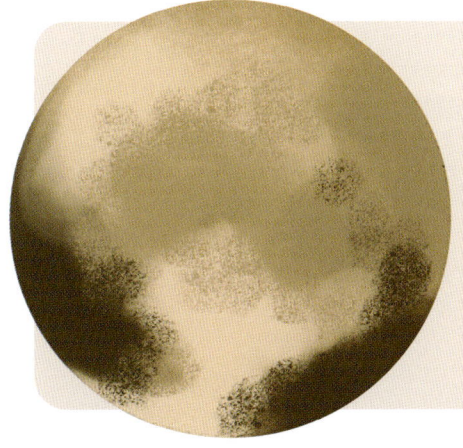

2015
The spacecraft New Horizons sent the first detailed **photos of Pluto** back to Earth.

2022
Russia invaded Ukraine. The conflict killed thousands of people and forced millions of Ukrainians to leave their homes. It caused worldwide disruption to grain and energy supplies.

THE MODERN WORLD

COVID-19

The worldwide pandemic of COVID-19 (the short name for Coronavirus Disease 2019) that began in 2020 was the worst since the flu of 1918–1919 (see page 97). In May 2023, The World Health Organization (WHO) said there had been nearly 766 million confirmed cases and 7 million deaths globally. First detected in China, it quickly spread around the world. Attempts to stop its spread came too late and were soon abandoned. Most nations then focused on slowing its spread, hoping to prevent health services being overwhelmed, and to buy time for a vaccine to be developed.

A NEW DISEASE

The first cases of a new **respiratory disease** emerged in China in late 2019. Caused by a **virus** carried in micro-aerosols (tiny particles that can stay airborne for a long time) in the air and large droplets on hands and surfaces, COVID-19 attacks people's lungs, causing coughing, fever, and other symptoms. It probably crossed to humans from pangolins or bats in or near a Chinese food market, or possibly came from a research laboratory, though we don't know for sure. The death rate from COVID-19 was high at first, particularly among older people and those who were already unwell in other ways, and were less able to fight the disease. Because people continued to travel when it first emerged, the virus spread quickly around the world and soon became a global pandemic.

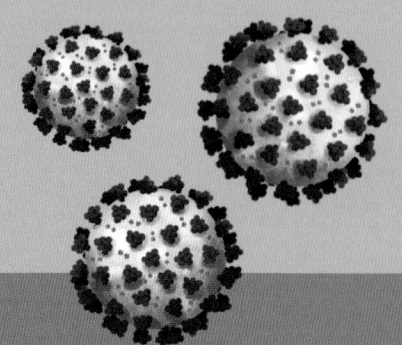

A WORLD CLOSED DOWN

Some countries closed their borders to foreign travel, but the disease had already taken hold and could only be slowed, not stopped. Many nations introduced **restrictions** forcing people to stay at home, to keep a safe distance from others, and to wear protective face masks when outside their homes. Movement was restricted: Schools, workplaces, and shops were closed, and gatherings of people were banned.

Cities were eerily empty, as people were not allowed outside without a good reason

THE MODERN WORLD

CRISIS IN CARE

In many countries, **hospitals could not cope** with the number of COVID patients needing care. Some ran out of oxygen and other vital supplies. Doctors and nurses also caught COVID, so there were fewer staff working in hospitals. In some places, such as China, new hospitals were built very quickly to provide more beds for people sick with COVID. In other places, people were looked after at home without specialist care.

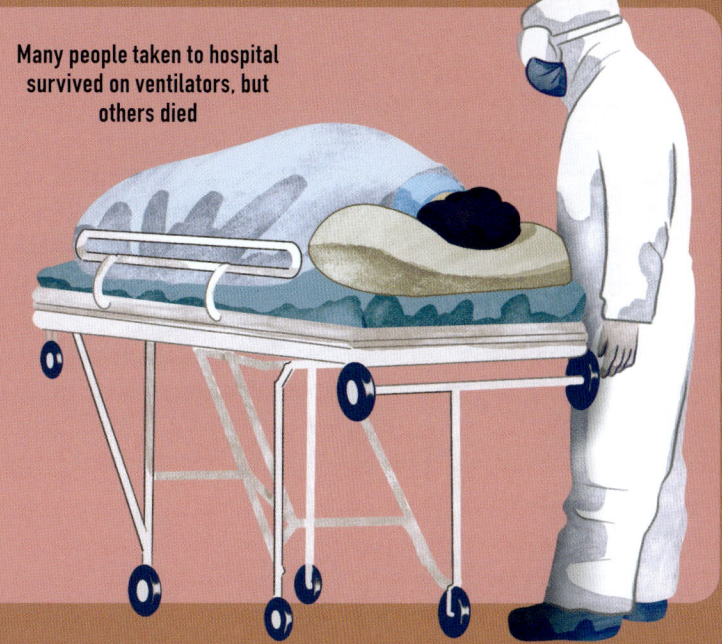

Many people taken to hospital survived on ventilators, but others died

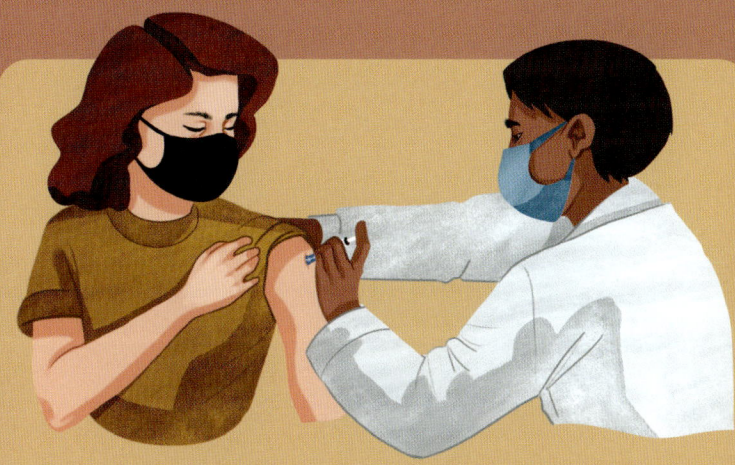

RACE FOR A VACCINE

Scientists immediately began trying to make a **vaccine** to prevent people developing serious symptoms from COVID-19. The first vaccines began to be used in late 2020. In many places, they were offered first to healthcare workers and the most vulnerable people. The vaccines offered some protection against getting COVID, but were most valuable in preventing serious illness or death in people who did catch it. By early 2023, an estimated 70 percent of the world's population had received at least one vaccination against COVID.

TRUTH AND ANTI-TRUTH

Many **conspiracy theories** grew up around COVID-19. Some people claimed either that the disease had been created in a laboratory and released deliberately or accidentally, or that the pandemic was a hoax and there was no such disease.

This highlighted the issues we have in the modern world with working out what is truth and what is not. With so many sources of information available, it can be difficult to find out what is really going on, especially since sometimes we are told "fake news" by people who want to influence us in some way. The emergence of AI technology is making this problem even more complicated, as well as raising many other questions.

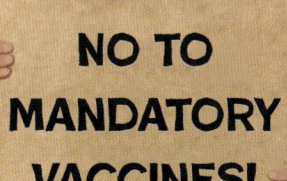

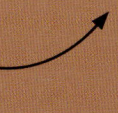

Some people objected to mandatory (when you have to do something) vaccines, to wearing a face mask, and to other measures designed to slow the spread of COVID-19

THE MODERN WORLD

FUTURE HISTORY

History doesn't just stop. Events are continuously happening that will later become history. These could be negative, such as global pandemics, wars, economic or political troubles, or natural disasters, or positive, such as scientific breakthroughs, increased international cooperation, or just everyday acts of kindness that change the world for the better. For now, you are living in the future's history.

CLIMATE IN CRISIS

People have known since the 1800s that increasing the amount of carbon dioxide in Earth's atmosphere could warm the planet. The evidence for **climate change** happening was clear by the late 20th century, but governments have been slow to take meaningful action. Already, higher average temperatures are causing more extreme weather events, droughts, floods, wildfires, crop failure, and melting ice. As temperatures rise worldwide, the areas we can live in comfortably will change, and people will have to move around or change how they live.

Melting ice at the Poles and in glaciers threatens to drown coastal cities

Hot and dry air makes wildfires more likely

Drought makes it hard to farm crops and animals

THE MODERN WORLD

RUNNING OUT

Earth has **limited supplies** of the things we need and use. Some of these are running out. To preserve valuable resources, we can reduce waste and recycle more. But people are also looking at new places to find some of the metals we need—under the ice, on the seabed, and even in outer space. One plan is to capture **asteroids** in space and mine them for the metals we need for our lifestyles. Future historians will know whether or not this becomes workable.

Will asteroids become the source of materials for our future phones and other items?

BEYOND EARTH

Humankind's voyage into **space** has only just begun. A crewed mission to Mars is likely in the near future, and at some point we will probably build bases on the Moon or Mars, or elsewhere. Some people believe humans will colonize other planets, but this would be a long way in the future. It's sometimes suggested as a solution to coping with worsening conditions on Earth. One day, our lives might be part of humankind's early Earth history while people have spread far and wide through space!

CONNECTED OR DISCONNECTED?

International problems in the 21st century have shown that in a connected world, everyone is threatened when things go wrong. Most countries depend on others for supplies—whether of food, fuel, or consumer goods. Disruption spreads far beyond one country's borders. The Russian invasion of Ukraine in 2022 caused global problems with food and fuel supplies. Rising nationalism has also led to some countries distancing themselves from others, hoping to protect their trade and borders with isolationist policies including a limit to immigration. The UK left the European trading bloc in 2021.

Many countries have ageing populations and need more workers, while others face war, climate change, and other problems that drive people overseas. These challenges seem to need **cooperation** to solve. Will the world become more or less connected in the future? Both have advantages and disadvantages.

LOOKING AHEAD

There are lots of problems in the world, but it's important to remember that humankind has faced very tough challenges before and survived. If we **pay attention to history**, we can learn lessons from the past and use them to help us take positive action in the present. One day, future historians will look back on the steps we took to address the issues facing us now and use that knowledge to help them with their own problems. Let's make our story one worth remembering!

Future historians might live in sustainable green cities

INDEX

A
Afghanistan 12, 14, 33, 38, 60, 85, 118, 121
Alexander the Great 32–3, 34
American Civil War 91
animals 10, 13, 14, 17, 18, 19, 23, 33, 35, 36, 44, 69, 91, 126
arts and crafts 9, 10, 11, 14, 24, 37, 43, 55
astronomy 19, 43, 58, 59, 75
Attila the Hun 45
Australia 10, 69, 72, 76, 80, 95, 96, 99, 122
Aztecs 64, 65, 71, 73

B
Babylon 19, 24, 25, 32, 34
Berlin Wall 113, 119
Black Death 49, 64, 65, 66–7, 127
boats and rafts 10, 22, 50, 55, 82, 99
bones 9, 10, 17, 21
bronze 12, 20, 22, 65

C
Caesar, Julius 38, 39, 41, 42
calendars 20, 39, 47, 75
cavalry 23, 37, 40, 99
cities 12, 13, 14, 15, 18, 19, 21, 22, 23, 24, 25, 30, 31, 33, 35, 38, 40, 42, 45, 46, 50, 55, 58, 59, 60, 62, 64, 70, 71, 72, 73, 75, 77, 80, 82–3, 86–7, 90, 96, 97, 102, 104, 106, 118, 122, 123, 124, 126
climate change 18, 22, 44, 122, 126–7
cloth and clothing 9, 31, 79, 83
Cold War 109, 112–13, 116, 118, 120
computers 115, 120
concentration camps 93, 103
Confucius 25, 36, 38, 75
copper 12, 23, 92
COVID-19 123, 124–5, 126
Crusades 49, 58, 59, 62

D
democracy 24, 27, 30–1, 94–5, 112, 114, 119
dictators and tyrants 20, 39, 41, 73, 106–7, 114, 115
diseases 11, 51, 56, 66–7, 69, 73, 84, 89, 92–3, 97, 100, 114, 118, 123, 124–5, 127,
dynasties 14, 19, 20–1, 23, 34, 36, 47, 54, 56, 57, 58, 59, 63, 65, 70, 73, 77, 90, 96

E
earthquakes 19, 20, 22, 46, 51, 56, 80, 96, 111, 121, 122
Egypt 12, 13, 14, 15, 16–17, 18, 22, 25, 27, 32–3, 34, 35, 37, 39, 50, 52, 62, 84, 91, 100

F
famines 18, 20, 22, 46, 61, 63, 64, 76, 85, 97, 101, 111, 121
farming 11, 12, 13, 26, 42, 50, 60, 67, 70, 74, 78, 82, 85, 86, 89, 91, 93, 100, 101, 111, 114, 126
food and crops 9, 11, 14, 26, 46, 54, 64, 67, 76, 78–9, 80, 82, 84, 85, 89, 92, 93, 95, 99, 101, 103, 104, 107, 109, 112, 124, 126–7

G
Genghis Khan 60–1, 62, 65
gladiators 35, 38
gold 24, 31, 34, 42, 46, 51, 55, 64, 92
government 20, 26–7, 46, 62, 81, 86–7, 93, 94, 97, 99, 100, 104, 105, 106, 111, 112, 114, 115, 118, 119, 121, 126
Great Wall of China 36, 65
gunpowder 43, 55, 81

H
health and medicine 16, 25, 44, 56, 83, 86, 89, 95, 105, 112, 123, 124–5

I
ice ages 10, 63, 70, 77
Indus Valley 12, 15, 17, 18, 53
Industrial Revolution 47, 80, 82–3, 86–7
iron 13, 22, 23, 55, 58, 63, 79, 82–3, 91, 101
Israel 14, 23, 39, 49, 52, 58, 60, 105, 115

J
Japan 11, 12, 27, 43, 46, 49, 51, 55, 56, 58, 61, 62, 63, 65, 74–5, 78, 80, 99, 100, 103, 104, 122,
Jerusalem 23, 39, 42, 49, 50, 51, 58, 59, 62
Jesus Christ 39, 42, 53,
Jewish people 31, 39, 47, 50, 52–3, 59, 102, 105, 115

M
maps 64, 76, 93
Mesoamerica 17, 37, 39, 64, 65
Mesopotamia 12, 16–17, 18, 19, 33
Mexico 12, 17, 19, 31, 45, 54, 64, 65, 73, 96
money 24, 57, 58, 67, 79, 85, 92, 100, 101, 122
Mongols 49, 59, 60–1, 62, 63, 64, 65, 66, 70
Muhammad 46, 47, 49, 50, 53
mummies 12, 15, 31
Muslims 46, 47, 49, 50, 51, 53, 54, 57, 58, 59, 60, 64, 72, 105, 109, 114, 115, 121, 122

N
North America, Indigenous peoples of 85, 89
numbers and numerals 10, 17, 35, 51

P
Palestine 50, 105, 115
paper 43, 56, 58, 100
Persia 25, 30, 32–3, 38, 52, 54, 59, 60
Peru 12, 13, 31, 37, 42, 71, 76, 118

Phoenicians 14, 22, 35
planets 19, 73, 77, 80, 117, 118, 121, 126–7
printing 43, 56, 65, 71
Punic Wars 35, 36, 38, 40
pyramids 13, 15, 22, 45, 54

R
railroads 91, 93
religion 19, 29, 34, 35, 46, 52–3, 75, 76, 118
   Buddhism 31, 35, 37, 39, 42, 46, 53, 56
   Catholicism 73, 77
   Christianity 39, 42, 44, 49, 52–3, 54, 56, 57, 58, 59, 72, 75, 76, 78, 97, 114
   Hinduism 19, 34, 53, 62, 105
   Islam 46, 47, 49, 51, 52–3, 54, 59, 64, 97, 100, 118, 121, 122, 123
   Judaism 51, 52–3
   Zoroastrianism 52

S
ships 22, 47, 50, 61, 70, 71, 72, 73, 74–5, 77, 78–9, 80, 82–3, 91, 93, 97, 99, 103
slavery 33, 35, 38, 50, 55, 56, 57, 69, 71, 73, 74, 77, 78–9, 81, 83, 84, 85, 86, 91, 92
South Africa 84, 105, 111, 120
space travel 110, 111, 115, 116–17, 118, 119, 121, 123, 127
stone 11, 13, 14, 15, 16, 17, 19, 22, 37, 51, 52, 63

T
temples 18, 23, 33, 39, 45, 51, 62, 65
terrorism 74, 81, 97, 101, 115, 118, 121, 122, 123
tools 9, 12, 13, 22, 26

V
Vikings 50, 55, 56, 57, 70
volcanoes 12, 19, 42, 46, 63, 76, 84, 85

W
warfare and weapons 12, 22, 23, 24, 26, 40, 49, 55, 61, 64, 81, 89, 90, 98–9, 102–3, 104, 107, 113
women 15, 27, 33, 50, 55, 57, 86–7, 94–5, 103, 110, 116
World Wars 89, 96, 97, 98–9, 100, 101, 102–3, 104, 109, 112, 116
writing 9, 16–17, 18, 19, 20–1, 22, 30, 31, 37, 43, 46, 52, 56, 58, 59, 60, 75